1984

Lemon Sky

Lemon Sky

A play by Lanford Wilson

A SPOTLIGHT DRAMABOOK
HILL & WANG   New York

For Jim and John

LEMON SKY was first presented on March 26, 1970, by Neal DuBrock at the Buffalo Studio Arena Theatre, Buffalo, New York, with the following cast:

ALAN   Christopher Walken
DOUGLAS Charles Durning
RONNIE   Bonnie Bartlett
PENNY   Kathryn Baumann
CAROL   Lee McCain
JERRY   Shawn McGill
JACK   Frank Martinez III

The production was directed by Warren Enters and designed by Stephen Henrickson. Lighting was designed by David Zierk.

The Buffalo Studio Arena Theatre production (with Steven Paul as JERRY and Willie Rook as JACK) was subsequently presented at the Playhouse Theatre, New York City, on May 17, 1970, produced by Haila Stoddard, Mark Wright, Duane Wilder, and Neal DuBrock. A staged reading of a working version of the play was given in the summer of 1968 at the Eugene O'Neill Theatre Foundation, Waterford, Connecticut.

Characters

ALAN, *29 now, 17 when he went to California.*

DOUGLAS, *his father.*

RONNIE, *his father's wife.*

PENNY ⎫
CAROL ⎭ *both 17, wards of the state, living with Douglas's family.*

JERRY ⎫ *Douglas and Ronnie's children, Alan's half brothers; 12*
JACK ⎭ *and 8.*

Time

Now and the late 1950's.

The Scene

One of the thousands of homes in the suburbs of San Diego, California. This one is in El Cajon, a city surrounded by low mountains. The home is more indicated than represented realistically. There is a back yard with redwood fences separating it from the neighbors', a low sloping roofline against a broad expanse of sky (which is never yellow); there are no walls but indicated divisions of rooms: a kitchen with a breakfast nook, refrigerator, stove, cabinets, etc.; the living room, carpeted, need only have a sofa and TV for furnishings; Alan's bedroom, upstage; and a garage with photographic printing equipment. There is furniture in an area of the yard and a garden against the redwood fence. The kitchen and an area indicating the bathroom may have tiled floors; a patio can be surfaced in redwood or concrete or flagstone. The stage area should be open and free. Sometimes the characters move down "halls" and into "rooms" and sometimes they cut across the entire stage, paying no attention to the room divisions.

There is no green in set or costumes; celadon, sage, anything else, but nothing green.

The lights move from area to area, defining our focus as well as the time of day and condition, and as many scenes as possible are bathed in a bright, cloudless sunlight.

Act One

(The stage is dark and undefined. All the characters are on stage, standing far upstage, just barely lighted. We should "feel" they are there without actually seeing them.)

ALAN

(Comes forward from the darkness. He is twenty-nine now. Thin and light, though not blond. Enthusiastic and pensive. He speaks rapidly and at times—when talking with the other characters—with a marked Midwestern accent. A little too preoccupied to begin a play, he enters a pool of light downstage and speaks to the audience.)

I've been trying to tell this story, to get it down, for a long time, for a number of years, seven years at least—closer to ten. I've had the title; I've had some of the scenes a dozen times, a dozen different ways, different starts. The times I've told it to friends as something I wanted to do, I've come home and tried to get it down—get to work on it—but the characters, the people ignored the damn story and talked about whatever they darn well pleased and wouldn't have any part of what I wanted them to say. They sat down to coffee or some damn thing.

The trouble was I wanted not to be the big deal, the hero, because I wasn't. No one was. Or how do I know who was? If it happened this way or that, who knows? But Dad—my dad—

(Quickly.)

If it's all autobiographical, so, I'm sorry, there it is; what can I tell you?

But how can I write about Dad? tell him? I knew him— lived with him—that I can remember, for six months.

(Quickly.)

I always say I lived in California for two years, because it sounds more romantic. Bumming around the beach a couple of years, on the Coast, it sounds great. Six months is like you didn't fit in. Like why bother? Like restlessness.

The title because—I don't know—it had something to do with

3

the state. California. I mean the nut fringe; first Brown, then
Reagan, and who knows what they'll come up—
(*Breaking off, returning to the thought above.*)
But finally I said, so if you're a hero; if you can't admit that
you weren't, if you've got to make a—if you can't admit that you
were really as big a bastard as everybody else, if you can't admit
that, for God's sake let it stay! And the fact that you can't will
say more about you than if you could. Leave it be! My father,
what do I know about him? If he's nothing—I mean *but nothing!*—then the fact that he comes off the short end of the stick
shows something. From that you know that there's *more* there.
You know? Leave it! Do it. Straight. Get it down, let it get
down and let it tell itself and *mirror*—by what you couldn't
say—what was really there.

DOUGLAS

(*Still in the shadows upstage; we cannot see him clearly. With
great emotion.*)
Hugged me! Hugged me, by God! By God, you can't! No matter what anybody anywhere says——

ALAN

(*Finishing the sentence, as if recalling a quote.*)
——you can't separate a kid from his father.

DOUGLAS

(*Just a bit more visible.*)
Even after—after this long a time. Even after this . . . time!

ALAN

Oh, God——

RONNIE

(*Faintly answering Doug. They begin to be visible.*)
I know, I know, Doug——

ALAN

(*Overlapping.*)
——what could I do? I got off the bus. I have a splitting headache from the altitude, from going over the Rockies and then
down to sea level—like a drop of ten thousand feet. Two and a

half days on a scenic-cruising Greyhound with faulty air-conditioning.

RONNIE

A migraine, he said, tension——

DOUGLAS

Well, yes, tension——

ALAN

(*Overlapping.*)

Finally I had to go to a doctor; after three days I could hardly talk. He said it was tension, the change in environment, just needed acclimatization and aspirin. Maybe it was—all I know is it started while I was in the Rockies or in Arizona: I woke up and my head was splitting. Like I wanted to die there, forget it. And with this headache—the bus pulled in and I—there's only one guy standing there. A very distinguished-looking man. I think, my God, he's so handsome, he's so good-looking, so young. In this dude suit. White dinner jacket—sport jacket, but white. Wool. Sun shining.

(*Sunlight beams around them.*)

And I said . . . Dad?

(*Douglas reaches out. Alan flies into his arms, quickly, then retreats.*)

I mean, what could I do? Shake his hand? But it was *right.* I felt it was right.

(*Then with immediate irritation.*)

No, Mother hadn't said anything against him—or at least what she said I was willing to forget. All the way back in the goddamned car——

DOUGLAS

(*Douglas is a strong gray-templed man of forty-five. Oddly romantic, childish and dogmatic, with great energy. Though considerably heavier than Alan, he is no taller, and there is a marked physical resemblance between the two. Douglas wears a white wool sport jacket and gray slacks. After he goes to work and comes back, we never see him dressed in anything but work or sport shirts again.*)

Now, I know she must have told you things about me, and she's
a good woman——

ALAN

(*To the audience. Cutting in.*)

I just wanted him not to feel bad—and not to think Mother had
said anything.

(*To Douglas.*)

Really.

DOUGLAS

Hell, I wanted you out here years ago.

ALAN

Sure, you don't have to think about it, Dad. Really. I don't hold
anything against you.

(*To the audience.*)

I almost wished I hadn't come. For a minute. It was *pain*ful!
His explanations! That was over, years ago—finished.

DOUGLAS

I know, but I had to say it.

ALAN

You don't have to think about it, Dad. Really, I don't.

DOUGLAS

(*Loosening up.*)

She's a good woman. But with a man like me—Al, she was at
me day and night with suspicions and limitations; I couldn't
breathe. All that—she didn't let a guy breathe.

ALAN

(*Distantly.*)

I understand, really.

DOUGLAS

Ronnie is different, a different kind of woman. She *lives*. You'll
love her.

ALAN

I'm anxious to meet her.

(*Half to the audience, half to Douglas.*)

And I have two brothers—half brothers—I've only seen once;
I hardly know them. Not at all.

6

DOUGLAS

You'll see them asleep—or tomorrow. I've got to go back for the second half of the day.

ALAN

(*To the audience.*)

He worked nights. The swing shift.

DOUGLAS

It pays better; not much, but it helps. You have the daytime to yourself; you work six hours instead of seven. I like to get out. You have some decent time to yourself. I just want you to understand.

RONNIE

(*Coming forward a step, extending her hand. She is small, attractive, blond and perhaps thirty-eight, with a good deal of taste and poise.*)

I was working in the garden——

ALAN

(*To the audience, suddenly.*)

If it was staged . . . I mean she knew Dad was coming to get me. He called to see if the bus was on time. He said he had waited only eight minutes——

DOUGLAS

Bulova——

ALAN

——so she——

DOUGLAS

——never wrong.

ALAN

——knew I'd be in at that time. What do you do? You meet a kid. Seventeen. Just out of high school. Your stepson, you've never seen before . . .

What are you going to be doing? What*ever* it is will make *some* kind of impression. You borrow a white sport coat to meet the kid, and you put on a pair of those thick, big white gloves, with dirt—from the *ground* dirt—on them, those white work

7

gloves with blue elastic wrists, big thick things for *men*, and—
(*Framing it.*)

—you are discovered in a garden hat so the California sun doesn't burn you and so you won't frown.

RONNIE

(*Coming forward a step.*)

I was working in the garden, pruning.

ALAN

(*To the audience.*)

Rose garden. The roses.

RONNIE

(*Showing him around the yard.*)

There's the bird of paradise; it's never going to bloom. I got it because it's Jack's favorite, the only flower he likes.

ALAN

(*Suddenly, wanting to hug them.*)

Jack! Jack! Little Jack!

RONNIE

Probably because it's very futuristic. "Spaceman" or "Jungleman."

ALAN

(*Back to framing the scene.*)

Pruning the roses. I hear the car drive into the driveway and the gate open at the side of the house. I turn around; I come across the back yard smiling.

RONNIE

(*Coming to him, taking off a glove, extending her hand.*)

Welcome, Alan, welcome. Hello.

ALAN

I take off a glove and extend my soft hand . . .

RONNIE

I was working in the garden, pruning.

ALAN

(*To the audience.*)

The roses. And a handshake; and Dad looks on beaming. *Beaming.* "You'll"——

8

DOUGLAS

You'll——

ALAN

——"love"——

DOUGLAS

——love——

ALAN

——"her."

DOUGLAS

——her.

ALAN

Blond hair. She looks like Blondie in the funnies; but she—you *do* love her. She's worried and planned and——

RONNIE

(*Cutting in.*)

Do you smoke? You want a cigarette?

ALAN

(*To the audience.*)

And of course you smoke, but you didn't know if you should and——

DOUGLAS

A beer?

ALAN

Yes, thanks, I didn't know——

DOUGLAS

Sure, take it, drink up. Hell, Carol drinks and worse, I think. You don't have to go on binges.

ALAN

I don't, no . . .

DOUGLAS

Ronnie smokes sometimes. About one a month.

RONNIE

Not that much even.

ALAN

(*To Ronnie and Douglas, with a marked Midwestern accent.*)

I've got this incredible headache; it's just the altitude. How high are we?

DOUGLAS

I don't know.

ALAN

Coming through the mountains . . .

RONNIE

You want some coffee?

DOUGLAS

Ronnie makes the best damn coffee in——
(*They move into the breakfast area, Alan sitting, Douglas leaning against the stove.*)

ALAN

Good.
(*Laughs, overwhelmed, nervous.*)
Good, yes . . .
(*To the audience, happy—without accent.*)
What do I say? Because I didn't *plan*. Because I didn't have a setting—it wasn't my house I was coming into. It *would be* mine, but I couldn't sit at the breakfast nook and pull up the ash tray and serve coffee out of the good cups like it was every day and lean against the stove and talk about work . . .

RONNIE

You look as I expected.

ALAN

(*When speaking with them, with the accent.*)
You look—do too—look like what I expected.

DOUGLAS

I've got to get along.

ALAN

How come?

RONNIE

Doug's on the night shift; so he has days off.

DOUGLAS

I still have to get in half a day.

ALAN

Good.

DOUGLAS

I told them if the bus was on time, I'd make it in; if you'd have been late, I'd have taken off.

ALAN

(*He has stood. Very joyously, throwing out his arms. Wildly.*) Where are they all!? Where is it?

(*Looking around, as though at the surrounding landscape.*)

A breakfast nook and out the kitchen window all the back yards are private, with redwood fences around them. Higher than your head. And mountains all around. Out the living-room window—Mount Capitan . . .

DOUGLAS

The big one, with the bald head, that's Mount Capitan.

RONNIE

(*Suddenly, quietly but urgently.*)

Alan, Mount McGinty is on fire, the whole sky—wake up, it's incredible——

DOUGLAS

(*Overlapping.*)

With the brush, Mount McGinty. And the blue one in the distance——

ALAN

——Mount Otay——

DOUGLAS

——behind that, Jerry would——

ALAN

(*Quickly to the audience.*)

My other brother.

DOUGLAS

——know that one; he knows them all.

(*Turning to look out the kitchen "window."*)

El Cajon Mountain, Cowles Mountain, and Mount Helix.

ALAN

Out the kitchen window, with a spotlighted cross on top and

expensive homes—but very expensive homes—built along the road that helixes up to the cross.

RONNIE

They turn the lights off at midnight.

ALAN

And the whole mountain disappears.

DOUGLAS

You can see it for miles.

RONNIE

We're surrounded.

DOUGLAS

Behind Mount Helix is La Mesa, the city of La Mesa, over on the other side; we can drive over there. Lemon Grove—they're all about the same. La Mesa—Grossmont may be a little more exclusive, a little more expensive.

ALAN

On the way here from downtown——

RONNIE

How do you like the traffic? Is that some drive?

ALAN

Yeah, that's something else, isn't it? I've never seen traffic like you've got here. I don't know if I'll want to drive or not.

DOUGLAS

Sure you will; you get used to it.

ALAN

But on the way out we must have passed a hundred houses that were going up. Half-constructed.

DOUGLAS

Across from the college they're building three hundred houses. Ranch types. A whole suburb. One guy.

(*Almost to the audience.*)

A whole city: shopping centers, two theatres—one regular and a drive-in—three hundred houses. Big ranch-type houses.

RONNIE

There's supposed to be four hundred new residents in California every day.

ALAN

Every day.

DOUGLAS

It's a big state, Al; it really is. Four hundred.

RONNIE

Every day.

DOUGLAS

Don't let anybody tell you the gold rush is over out here, boy.

ALAN

I guess not.

DOUGLAS

Guys are making a killing out here.

ALAN

And the climate, I suppose——

DOUGLAS

(*A brief concession.*)

March is a mess. Late March into April—it rains, but that's about it for the whole year. And it's a little cooler, but outside of that——

ALAN

I don't suppose you get any——

RONNIE

(*Both are shaking their heads, seriously, not ironically.*)

No, no snow——

DOUGLAS

Very little; up in the mountains——

RONNIE

——It seldom even freezes. Up in the mountains. The Lagunas and higher. We drive up or else the boys would never have seen snow. Of course you don't see it falling, which is half the treat. It falls during the night. It'll snow a foot and then thaw within two days.

ALAN

A foot? Overnight?

RONNIE

A lot more, sometimes.

ALAN

That's going-to-hell snowin'.

DOUGLAS

Alan, you'll love it. It's heaven. I mean it's really heaven. You'll love it here.

RONNIE

We hope you do.

DOUGLAS

You will! Hell! By God, anybody who wouldn't, sumpin's wrong with 'em er sumpin, huh?

ALAN

I think there'd have to be. I do already. We were coming through New Mexico and I didn't believe it . . . the air-conditioning wasn't working. Of course, who needs it in Nebraska? But by the time we get to El Centro, it's burning hot. Your first stop in California: El Centro. What do you do your first stop in California? You buy a glass of orange juice. Never. Whatever you do, never buy orange juice at the Greyhound bus station in El Centro, California. Yeahhh! God-awful. The worst. The worst single paper cup of orange juice I've ever had in my life.

(*To the audience by now, as well as to Ronnie and Douglas.*)

It's not native to El Centro. Oranges can't grow there. Gila monsters you could buy. Navajo blankets, moccasins, turquoise earrings, Apache tears, you can buy. That's it. Of course, even getting to El Centro is a nightmare. You know California, you've seen the pictures: palm trees, sunsets, swimming pools, oceans, and mountain springs. The first five hours—five and a half—you are treated to the world's most barren desolation: the Mojave Desert. Telephone poles are stuck in a big hunk of asphalt to hold them upright. The asphalt is boiling. You think: this is California! Oh, wow, who does the public relations on this place!

(*Back to them, exaggerating.*)

It's a hundred and five degrees! It's March! I want you to know.

14

March—and it's a hundred and five. In Nebraska it's forty-seven and it's a warm day when I left.

RONNIE

I know, I remember.

DOUGLAS

She worked there.

ALAN

(*To the audience, rather a different mood, straight, low; no accent.*)

What I've heard about Ronnie is Dad met her and dated her—he was still married—sometime during that time he was still married to Mother.

DOUGLAS

In Lincoln. Private secretary to the attorney of the state. State attorney, same difference, huh?

ALAN

(*Continuing.*)

And maybe they came out here together, maybe not. He said he'd send for us—Mother and me. He ran off, out to here. O.K. She never blamed him.

RONNIE

A wonderful man, and an interesting job.

ALAN

You take shorthand and all that, then?

RONNIE

Oh, yes. I want to forget it. It's like riding a bicycle; you can't. They let the secretaries run the country, I think. From my experience.

ALAN

Probably they do.

DOUGLAS

I've got to get along.

ALAN

How come?

RONNIE

Doug's on the night shift; so he has days off.

DOUGLAS
So I can get in half a day yet.

ALAN
Good.

DOUGLAS
You darn-betcha.

ALAN
Yeah.
(*Laughs.*)

DOUGLAS
(*Embarrassingly straight and serious.*)
I can't tell you how much I've wanted you here.

RONNIE
(*Soberly.*)
He has, Alan.

DOUGLAS
I tried. I wrote once or twice, but your mother thought I was trying to kidnap you or some damn thing. She wouldn't let you come.

RONNIE
He cried. It's the only time I've ever seen——

ALAN
(*To the audience—cutting it off.*)
He said he had to go, he worked on the night shift, he could get in half a day yet. That it was great having me here. Finally. He'd dreamed about it.

RONNIE
(*They have moved from the kitchen. Showing him around.*)
That's going to be your room.

ALAN
Great.

DOUGLAS
(*Returning to previous. Soberly.*)
So bad. I can't tell you.

ALAN
(*Soberly.*)

I'm glad to be here. I am.

RONNIE

The patio, it will go here; you've seen the garden. The living room, the TV—it's in the cabinet; I can't stand a naked eye staring at me. We almost never watch it. Doug watches the fights and the ball games in the afternoons.

ALAN

That's right, I can watch the games.

DOUGLAS

(*Showing him around.*)

That's the darkroom.

ALAN

Wow. I didn't know that.

DOUGLAS

The mounted picture there, the second one, I won an award on last year. It's taken actually with a red filter looking straight into the sun like that—it's called sunspot—that's the sun here and the reflection here, the way the sun hits the water. It's a bitch of a shot to make because of the glare. The reflection. You have to use a filter, have to know what you're doing.

(*Slapping the table.*)

That's a professional enlarger; that's as good as they make them.

RONNIE

Doug went through a woodworking phase about five years ago, so we have a table saw and a lathe and all of that. He'll build the patio this summer.

DOUGLAS

Not by myself I won't. Not now that I have help.

ALAN

Right. I'd love to.

RONNIE

Dad's workroom you've seen.

ALAN

Do you develop your own film?

DOUGLAS

Develop, print, enlarge to any size, all in the same room—the

whole works. It's not difficult—it's goddamned exacting; everything's timed pretty close. You have to know what the hell
you're doing.

RONNIE

(*Pointing out.*)

Mount Helix with the cross, and Mount Otay; isn't that god-
awful? Over there—nearly in Mexico.

ALAN

All around. It's beautiful.

DOUGLAS

You'll love it.

ALAN

(*Enthralled.*)

I do. I do. I do.

DOUGLAS

(*Suddenly serious. Man-to-man.*)

Carol . . . Now, I want you to know, don't be embarrassed.
We have these two girls living here.

(*The girls can be seen dimly in the distance.*)

ALAN

You wrote me; I know.

DOUGLAS

Well, Alan, they're wards of the state. They've had terrible
lives; you don't know——

ALAN

Maybe I——

DOUGLAS

——Just terrible; you don't know. Penny's father left her, her
mother died, she's lived in one bad foster home after another.
They're happy here. The woman said we were one of the best
homes in San Diego County. They live here like it's their home.

RONNIE

They really do.

DOUGLAS

They've been here—Penny a year, Carol a year now and a half.
It's their home and we all get along like a family.

RONNIE

You'll have Carol's room and she can sleep with——

DOUGLAS

And Carol . . . her mother and father both died when she was too young to remember it——

RONNIE

She does, though.

DOUGLAS

She says she doesn't. Penny's good. She gets along fine. Carol. I want to talk to you man-to-man. Alan, Carol is a whore. She's promiscuous. She came here bragging she'd slept with six sailors in one night once.

RONNIE

Seven, but one more or less.

(*Alan laughs.*)

DOUGLAS

She has a boyfriend now; she's trying to straighten out. Hell, she was on pills, she was on God knows what. Things I hadn't even heard of.

RONNIE

But she dates this guy regularly now; he's a darn nice guy. You'll meet him.

DOUGLAS

You have to treat her like—think of her like a sister. We can't have you——

ALAN

O.K., I won't.

DOUGLAS

It's important.

ALAN

How can you keep them? They must cost . . .

DOUGLAS

Well, the state sends us sixty dollars a month toward their board——

RONNIE

It's not as much as they eat, even. But we make a home for them.

19

ALAN

(*Joyous.*)

Where are they? Penny! Carol! Jerry! Jack! Jerry's twelve and is a little me. A little blond me, only fatter. A little. Jack's a brush ape. A—a—renegade. Jerry and I look a little alike; Jack takes after Ronnie, except for his eyes. Penny's a dope. She's great. But she's a dope. Carol's gorgeous!

RONNIE

Not really; she's attractive. Striking. She could be a model. She has that kind of figure. Beautiful skin.

DOUGLAS

Not really, though. She knows how to fix herself up is all. She's a come-on. She's not got a personality. She's neurotic. She's had a terrible life, Alan; you don't know.

(*Suddenly messing his hair.*)

Fella! Devil!

(*To the audience, hugging Alan's head against him. Proudly.*)

I mean he was my kid. He looked like me. More than Jerry ever thought about. When I was his age. I was skinny like that. I had to work out.

(*To Alan.*)

I could never gain weight. But God . . . !

RONNIE

When we were married——

DOUGLAS

I put on weight the first week. It's the air. You will, too. And Ronnie's a good cook.

ALAN

Good.

RONNIE

Which reminds me, are you hungry?

DOUGLAS

(*Seriously.*)

They've gone out. We wanted them to, so we could meet you. Get to know each other a little first. The boys are staying with Mildred. I imagine they'll be asleep when she brings them home tonight. We told them they'd see you in the morning. One more day won't matter—you'll be here awhile. Penny'll be in. She went to a movie with Rose, I imagine.

RONNIE

Rose you've got to meet. She's unbelievable. Are you sure you can't eat?

ALAN

Really.

(*To the audience.*)

I've got this incredible headache; a migraine, only I don't know it, and I've not had one since. Three days it lasted—all through that first day and night. It can't go on like this, of course; there'll be a scene soon. Dad had to go to work; he could get in half a day—night—yet. He always called it day . . . the working day.

DOUGLAS

I want you to go down there. You can get a job if you're going to be going to school. It costs, you know.

ALAN

I wanted to work somewhere, to pay my way——

DOUGLAS

I wish to God we could——

RONNIE

——afford to pay your way.

DOUGLAS

Alan, we can't; we just can't. I want to, but we can't that much. We'll help, sure, all we can——

ALAN

No, I want to. I said I would.

DOUGLAS

Hell, it's healthy. Everybody out at State is working part time, anyway. Earn their keep. We'll have to get you a car, won't we? You drive?

ALAN

Yeah, fairly well.

DOUGLAS

Get you a little Austin or one of those. What'd you think?

ALAN

(*To the audience and them.*)

What can I say? I think it's great.

DOUGLAS

We'll go over and look; you gotta have it to get you to school, doncha? I'm not going to squire you in; you don't want to have to take a bus every morning. Huh?

ALAN

(*To the audience.*)

There'll be a scene. Those who are confused will say, thank God, something to watch; maybe everyone will stop flying around.

(*Douglas stands a moment watching, then turns with a proud smile and exits.*)

RONNIE

I guess you'll want to get some sleep soon.

ALAN

Before too long. I couldn't sleep on the bus. I almost broke my neck.

RONNIE

You want to go right now?

ALAN

No, no.

RONNIE

Whenever you're ready.

ALAN

Could I have another coffee?

RONNIE

(*She pours another coffee.*)

He's talked about you so much. I didn't know about you at all when we were married. He told me the first night; it was quite a shock. I didn't even know he had been married. He cried. He said he wanted to bring you out here, and I wanted you too. But your mother—and she was right, don't you think?

ALAN

Yes.

(*To the audience.*)

What could——

RONNIE

It's better this way. You're not torn apart, half in one place and half in another. He missed you so much. That's why he wanted to have another kid right away. You're not shocked or embarrassed or anything, me speaking with you frankly?

ALAN

No, God, no; it's a relief.

RONNIE

Good. I've so looked forward to knowing you. Doug's mother gives us pretty regular reports about you.

ALAN

She does?

RONNIE

Oh, sure. That's why we asked you out. She said you were out of high school; she thought it was about time you saw some of the country—and that you and Doug got reacquainted.

ALAN

She knew I wanted to go on to school.

RONNIE

What are you going to study?

ALAN

You know, I don't have any idea. Liberal Arts—I don't know.

RONNIE

There's time. We'll take you up to San Diego State so you can get registered; it's a beautiful campus. Don't decide for awhile. . . . Jack has a birthday party coming up—his eighth. Two dozen local hellions. You'll want to escape from that, I imagine. Maybe you can take Jerry to a movie or something. He considers himself much too adult for that crowd.

ALAN

Of course—he's eleven.

RONNIE

No, please. Twelve. And a half: he stretches it a little; he was born Christmas Day. You knew that.

ALAN

Yes. But that's all.

(*To the audience; a marked contrast as he drops the accent.*) I'd seen them just once, five years ago; Jack was three, Jerry seven. Dad and the kids came to town, and it was arranged that if a friend of Mother's went along, we'd all go to the zoo in Omaha; and we had a picnic which I remember as the most horrible experience of my younger life. Everyone worried about how I was going to react, and me not knowing what was happening. Just I didn't want any of it and I couldn't get it through my head how any of these people could be related to me. And I was freezing to death, which is all I really remember: it was November and all the animals had their winter coats and were ugly, anyway.

RONNIE

(*Standing, whispering—stage whisper.*) You want to see them?

(*They walk to between the boys' beds.*)

ALAN

(*Same whisper.*) Don't wake——

RONNIE

No, you'll meet them in the morning. Jerry. He has asthma and snores like a tank. Of course, Jack could sleep through anything.

ALAN

(*Whisper.*) He's cute.

RONNIE

(*Whisper.*) Well, of course he's cute. He looks like me. He's the hairy one. He takes that from my brother; look at those arms. He has hair like that all over him.

ALAN

(*Whisper—to the audience.*)

Blond, like a white—a little white orangutan or something.

(*Penny comes in the front entrance, walks to the refrigerator door, opens it, and stands in front of it. Penny is nearly eighteen; she is slow and dull moving and almost heartbreakingly unattractive.*)

RONNIE

(*Hearing the noise.*)

That's Penny.

ALAN

(*Beginning in whisper and changing into regular voice as they move out of the boys' area.*)

Penny, on whom the plot will pivot, such as it is. On Penny and a photograph taken my first day in California and my first day at the ocean. First ocean, the Pacific. Real salt; I almost hadn't believed it. I had to go taste it to be sure. Jerry on one side, me in the middle, Jack on the other. A picture of the three grandchildren to send to my grandmother.

RONNIE

Doug's mother wrote back and said she couldn't believe it. That wasn't Alan between those two kids; that was Doug when he was seventeen.

ALAN

Really?

RONNIE

Oh, now he's very distinguished, very proud of the mustache and the graying temples. The whole image; the white jacket.

ALAN

(*To the audience.*)

He had borrowed it from a friend, but he liked it; it suited him. And it did. So he bought it from the guy.

PENNY

(*They come to her. Still with the refrigerator door open.*)

Pleased to meet you. I've heard a lot about you.

ALAN

(*To the audience.*)

And I feel like I should bow.

(*To Penny.*)

They didn't know a thing. It was all conjecture.

RONNIE

Penny's a science major and very serious about it.

PENNY

Well, I'm not that serious about——

ALAN

What do you want to do with——

PENNY

Oh, well, I'll probably teach.

(*Dead pause.*)

I like kids. I guess.

ALAN

I couldn't be a teacher if they paid me, and I understand they don't.

PENNY

California's not bad. They pay well here.

ALAN

I guess I've heard that.

RONNIE

Do you want something to eat?

PENNY

(*Closing the refrigerator door.*)

No. I've got to go to bed.

RONNIE

Did you see Rose?

PENNY

Uhm. She's given up politics; she's learning to play the guitar.

(*Alan laughs.*)

RONNIE

Penny dates the best-looking boy at the college.

PENNY

(*Pause.*)

He really is.
(*Shrug.*)

RONNIE

He's a tennis pro.

PENNY

Not pro.

RONNIE

Well, not pro, but he will be.

PENNY

He was in the Olympics.

ALAN

They play tennis in the Olympics?

PENNY

Oh, sure. Or maybe it was skiing, because he skis. His dad's
got a lodge in Colorado. Carol and I are—Carol and me—damn
—Carol and I!—are both going with millionaires. Not really, but
they have a lot of money. Phil drives a Pontiac convertible. It's
so beautiful, I feel stupid driving around in it—especially the
way he drives.

RONNIE

Why, how does he drive?

PENNY

I don't know. Conspicuously. I mean the top's never up unless
it's raining. Even in the middle of winter. I've had a cold since
I've known him. Do you mind if I go on to bed?

ALAN

No, if you're sleepy.

PENNY

'Cause I am.

ALAN

I can see you tomorrow.

PENNY

Good night, Alan. Ronnie, is Carol in yet?

RONNIE

No. God knows, she's out with Sonny.

PENNY

Good night.

(*Exits to bedroom.*)

ALAN

And that's all of Penny that night. That first night. That was it. But more, there's more.

RONNIE

I want to tell you about Carol. It's terrible.

ALAN

(*To the audience.*)

Now this is funny. . . . I sat there sober-faced and believed every word.

RONNIE

(*To the audience.*)

Well, I had to tell him something, right? I mean the girl is a whore. Let's face it: she's a nice kid but she's sick. With Sonny, Sonny is religious—that much is true.

ALAN

(*He leans against the counter and watches, smiling, listening to a favorite family joke.*)

Go on, go on . . .

RONNIE

(*To the audience.*)

Well, I didn't know if he'd believe it or not; what do I know? He's seventeen; my boys are twelve and eight. But if I didn't say something that first night, then Carol would have him seduced by the next afternoon. So I told him she had this incurable "disease," that wasn't painful, but it was an impossible disgrace. I said they were trying to cure it, but it was only fifty-fifty.

ALAN

Trichinosis.

RONNIE

Well, I couldn't think of a medical-sounding name that I thought I could remember. When did you know?

28

ALAN

Not for years. You can lie to me; I'll believe anything.

RONNIE

Of course, I didn't know if he'd buy it or not.

ALAN

I said trichinosis was something you got from eating pork.

RONNIE

(Seriously, to him.)

Well, *one* kind.

ALAN

She said this was a different kind; it was similar, but much worse.

RONNIE

(Seriously, to him.)

And very rare.

(To the audience.)

I thought with all those sailors he might believe she could have gotten anything. And it doesn't show up on the boy. But he passes——

ALAN

(To her.)

He's a carrier.

RONNIE

Right. And he passes it on to the next girl, who might be some-one he likes very much, Alan. And respects. And——

ALAN

And I bought that.

RONNIE

(To the audience.)

And I said she wasn't sleeping with Sonny, which was true as far as any of us knew.

CAROL

(From the shadows.)

It was true.

RONNIE

(Reassuringly, to her, quickly.)

No, we knew. Anyway, I described it dreadfully. All the symptoms.

ALAN

(*To the audience.*)

And all the time I have this pounding headache I'm practically fainting from.

RONNIE

Well, who would know? You didn't show it.

ALAN

(*To the audience and her.*)

I have this smile plastered on my kisser, and this look of concern. I didn't care if this girl had last-stage syphilis. I was dying there in the middle of the kitchen my first night.

RONNIE

Anyway, I made poor Carol sound like a very unattractive sleeping arrangement.

CAROL

And of course I was going balmy because I thought, why isn't anything working with this guy? Why isn't he turning on to me? How should I know he thinks I'm Typhoid Mary? I'm coming on like the Army and Navy Band with about sixty colors flying, and this cat's outrunning ostriches in the other direction. I changed toothpaste. I did, I changed my toothpaste. Twice.

RONNIE

(*Suddenly very sober.*)

Doug used to talk about you.

ALAN

I was only five.

RONNIE

I know, but he loves children. Sometimes I think Doug should have had a girl. He'd have been a better father to her. You should see him with the neighbor girls. He really loves them.

(*Long pause.*)

ALAN

(*To the audience.*)

I didn't tell her that I had a sister. I thought about it, but I didn't say anything. That's what I was thinking about—a lot that first night.

RONNIE

No, you didn't.

ALAN

(*To the audience.*)

I'd had a sister who was born dead; it would have been Dad's only daughter. He was out every night until God knows what hour. He would come in with lipstick all over his shirt—and mother was pregnant—and he'd swear it was someone's sister, and mother would check his story and the guy wouldn't even have a sister—like he didn't even bother to make the story convincing, and then he'd rage at her for not believing him and spying behind his back. That's what he meant by "at him." Snooping at his heels all the time.

So mother got her labor pains one night when he was out and she was walking the floor. This was eight months along only. And she called a friend of Dad's to ask if he knew where Dad was and—this guy's name was Carl. So Carl and his wife drove mother to the hospital, and the baby was born dead. Stillborn. Mom said she didn't much care at the time. It wasn't even buried—they don't—they consider it never lived.

(*Pause.*)

I don't know. I know Carl beat the shit out of Dad, and right after that Dad left. So if Ronnie thought he was guilty about leaving *me*—or wanted another *son*—probably not.

RONNIE

He wasn't going with me.

ALAN

Even if he was, you didn't know.

RONNIE

It was a full year after that that we——

ALAN

(*Removed, uninterested.*)

He'd been in California a year. He'd met Ronnie, but he came

back afterwards and dated her; that's when they went together a year, after he'd already left. She said. I didn't ask Dad. It doesn't matter. Anyway, that's what I was thinking—or, rather, trying not to think—that night. And trying not to blame him. (*Pause.*)
She would have been four years younger than me.

RONNIE

Thirteen.

ALAN

Well. What time is it? It must be after midnight.

RONNIE

Are you kidding? It's one thirty or after. We talked for three hours straight.

ALAN

Briefing me on the neighborhood. Ronnie was the neighborhood confessor. Since she didn't give a wild flying damn what anyone did and didn't gossip, she got all the juiciest stories.

RONNIE

It's always been like that.

ALAN

And I liked you very much. Which is no mean trick for a stepmother.

RONNIE

And you told me about Doug being in jail.

ALAN

How did I——

RONNIE

We were just talking about anything, and you asked——

ALAN

(*With an accent.*)
Is Dad still interested in drawing and painting? Grandma's attic is full of stuff he did.

RONNIE

The paintings of boats and all the airplanes? I think he's always been crazy about airplanes. No, he doesn't do that any more.

ALAN

I used to go up and look at them every time I went there.

RONNIE

Well . . . he builds things . . . and you saw all the photographic equipment. I think he must have stopped painting when he was a teen-ager.

ALAN

Yes, I think Mother said he did them when he was in jail.

RONNIE

(*Beat.*)

When he was where?

ALAN

Didn't you know that? I wouldn't want to——

RONNIE

No, it's O.K. What?

ALAN

Well, he was in on a—not a robbery but a burglary of a house with some guys when he was sixteen, and went not actually to a jail but to a reform school for a year. And that's when he did those— It was a long time ago; I guess it isn't anything necessarily that he should have told you.

RONNIE

Or that you should have been told, for that matter.

ALAN

I'm sorry; I wouldn't have——

RONNIE

No, it doesn't matter. I asked you.

(*To the audience.*)

And he was so damned honest—I could have clubbed him.

ALAN

(*To the audience.*)

I was. I was.

RONNIE

You want to go to bed, don't you?

ALAN

I think so.

RONNIE
It's after two.

ALAN
I'm falling on my face.

RONNIE
Go on to bed; it's all right.

ALAN
Are you going to wait up for Dad?

RONNIE
No, no, he doesn't expect you to wait up. You won't need more covers than that.

ALAN
No, not here.
(He laughs, sits on the bed, and tucks under.)

RONNIE
Good night, Alan.

ALAN
I'll see you tomorrow.

RONNIE
I won't wake you; Doug gets up early; he never sleeps more than four or five hours.

ALAN
Good lord.

RONNIE
I know; don't worry, we'll let you sleep. Tomorrow anyway. Everyone keeps their own hours.
(Carol approaches the front door.)

ALAN
Right.

RONNIE
(Turning to the front, leaving him.)
Speaking of which.

CAROL
(Entering. She will soon be eighteen; tall, very thin; smashingly attractive, and quite a wreck.)

34

I know, it's late; I wasn't watching. Where's Alan? Did he come?

RONNIE

Yes, he came.

CAROL

Doug here?

RONNIE

He went on to work.

CAROL

Went to *work?* Well, of course, he went to work, Carol. What'd you think, he stayed here with his son? How's Alan?

RONNIE

Very nice. But that isn't the subject.

CAROL

Oh, Christ, Ronnie, don't start!

RONNIE

It's two o'clock.

CAROL

(*Looks at her watch, puts it to her ear, shakes her arm during speech.*)
It isn't any—well, my watch's stopped. Damn.

RONNIE

You know I don't care, but they ask.

CAROL

We've been sitting out in front for over an hour. Didn't you hear us drive up? I thought I saw you at the window.

RONNIE

Carol, I don't care.

CAROL

Well, neither do I. He was so sweet.

RONNIE

I like Sonny.

CAROL

We talked.
(*Partly to the audience.*)

35

Sonny's dad has a ranch in Texas—over twenty thousand acres, which he says is small. That's probably larger than Rhode Island. And they raise Herefords and houses and oil, and have about half the money in the country and investments everywhere. His mom and dad are paralyzed over what's going on in Cuba; apparently they own it.

RONNIE

Anyway, be that as it may, I've a vivid imagination, but it fails me when I try to conjure up what you do until——

CAROL

(*Cutting in violently.*)

Oh, Ronnie, would you stop it! Just stop it already! No, he doesn't lay me; no, never, not once. Look at my hands, for God's sake! You think I can stand it?

(*Exposing her hands, which are bloody on the palms.*)

RONNIE

Good God, what's wrong with——

CAROL

Well, it isn't stigmata; you can count on that! Sonny is Catholic with a vengeance, and I've never thought I could be in love with anyone. There it is!

(*Rather to the audience.*)

Carol's problem; never thought she could cut it, and I am—very much in love with a rich Texan Catholic, and he has land, lots of land, and principles that I never even knew were principles. And I used to take "downs"; but pills are wrong, of course, so I promised him I wouldn't take them any more. No, we no longer live in a yellow submarine; we live on a red perch. And he makes out so damn beautifully, and I can't ask *him* and I can't be "bad"—his word, not mine—and I can't calm down with the pills and I claw my *hands*, the palms of my hands, apart.

(*Totally breaking off—disgusted with herself.*)

Well, shit, Carol, there's no sense in causing a war about it. I cut them down yesterday; I'll cut them off tonight. But that won't help, because I'll bite my lip or something else if I can't get a hold of something to take to calm my damned frazzled——

RONNIE

Carol, I'm very lenient and I know you can wrap me around your little finger; I know you've had to do that in order to get anything——

CAROL

Don't make excuses for me, for God's——

RONNIE

Carol, I want to say something. I know you want to stay here for the next eight or whatever months, until you're eighteen, and I want you here; but if I see one pill, one of your tranquilizers, I'll report it. It's something I can't tolerate. I have two young sons here and I can't risk them taking something by mistake——

CAROL

(*Overlapping.*)
You don't have to tell me that. Do you think Sonny would stand for it? He's a lot better police dog than—a LOT better police dog than you, believe me——

RONNIE

There've been two different cases in the last year of kids being poisoned by taking their mother's barbiturates or someone's who had left them around the house. If I know you're taking them, I'll feel obliged to tell Sonny as well as the welfare——

CAROL

(*Screaming.*)
You don't have to tell anybody any goddamned thing! Because I PROMISED him; you know what that MEANS?
(*Regains her control; holding her hands.*)
That I didn't need them.

RONNIE

Do your hands hurt?

CAROL

Yes, they hurt like fire.

RONNIE

Let me put something——

CAROL

Oh, I'll do it; you're supposed to be bawling me out. You *can't*, Ronnie. I can get out of anything; I'm a master.

RONNIE

You're also a mess.

CAROL

You're telling me.

RONNIE

Let me put something on you.

CAROL

(*Hotly.*)

No, dammit; you're not going to stain me up with iodine, thanks.

RONNIE

I'll put some salve on them, not iodine.

CAROL

They're not that bad, really. I'll do it. Are you waiting up for Doug?

RONNIE

No. He'll be in.

CAROL

Alan's in my room?

RONNIE

For tonight. We'll arrange something.

CAROL

Just let me flop somewhere.

RONNIE

Put something on your hands, that salve.

CAROL

O.K. Good night.

RONNIE

Carol. Don't.

(*Pause.*)
Don't stay out this late. They want you in by twelve.

CAROL

I won't, Ronnie. You're great. I'm sorry; I won't.
(*Kisses her on the cheek.*)

RONNIE

(*To the audience.*)
She will, and I can't blame her, of course. He's the only thing
she's got—Sonny. She's on probation with the state and us and
Sonny, too.

CAROL

So, I'm used to it. Don't make me out a martyr. I hate it. Besides,
I can do it better. I haven't even got started on my mom and dad
and poor upbringing and what a rotten life I've had. Besides,
I'm a nymphomaniac—coupled with a for-all-practical-purposes
eunuch in the shape of a Greek god.

RONNIE

Which isn't necessary with you, but it doesn't hurt anything.

CAROL

It hurts. It hurts. Everything. All over. Good night.
(*She goes off to the girls' bedroom. Ronnie stands a moment,
then goes off to her bedroom. The stage is empty for a few seconds, then Douglas enters, goes to the kitchen, opens a can of
beer, takes a hunk of cheese, looks into the girls' bedroom, then
Alan's, and exits into his own bedroom as the lights fade to a
deep midnight blue. All is quiet for a beat, then a very slow
dawn. At a nice bright sunshine the lights hold. Jerry stirs in
his bed and sits up suddenly. Jumps up and sneaks down to
Alan's room. Creeps in and shakes him gently.*)

JERRY

Alan?
(*Sits on the side of the bed, waits.*)
Alan? Are you awake?

ALAN

(*Stirring.*)

Huh?
(*The scene is whispered.*)

JERRY

Good morning.

ALAN

Good morning. Is it morning?

JERRY

Almost.

ALAN

Do you always get up this early?

JERRY

I woke up.

ALAN

It isn't daylight yet, is it?

JERRY

Oh, yeah.
(*Starts to window to pull the shades up.*)
It's Sunday, it's real bright out——

ALAN

NO! I believe you. That's O.K.
(*Smiling, focusing on him now.*)
Are you Jerry or Jack?

JERRY

Don't you know?

ALAN

Yes. You're Jerry.

JERRY

Jack's asleep.

ALAN

And let's see; you would be twelve and a half, right?

JERRY

Right. I'll be thirteen——

ALAN

Christmas Day.

JERRY

Right. What's the matter with your head?

ALAN

I don't know; only it's splitting wide open. It has been all night
—ever since we crossed New Mexico. I think it has something
to do with the altitude. Are we at sea level?

JERRY

No, one thousand three hundred eighty feet. That's Mount
Helix.

ALAN

How do you know? Are you studying geography?

JERRY

No, there's a sign on the highway. Do you want some aspirin?

ALAN

Where's the highway?

JERRY

About two blocks from here.

ALAN

Oh. Do you have any, do you think?

JERRY

What?

ALAN

Aspirin.

JERRY

Oh, I thought you meant highways, did I have any highways——

ALAN

No, aspirin——

JERRY

I'll get you one.

ALAN

Could you? Bring me three if you have plenty.

JERRY

(Has run out; returns.)

You shouldn't take more than one.

ALAN

Huh? Oh, it's O.K., honey; I always take three. Two doesn't
do any good and four makes me sick.

JERRY

O.K.

(*As water runs.*)

ALAN

(*Calling.*)

What time is it, Jerry?

JERRY

It's seven o'clock already.

ALAN

(*Flops down in bed.*)

Oh, God. Jerry, I didn't get to bed till three or something.

JERRY

(*Re-entering.*)

Do adults need eight hours sleep?

ALAN

(*Between aspirins.*)

Eight or ten.

JERRY

Dad says he can't sleep but four hours. He says you shouldn't.

ALAN

Then why do I feel like this?

JERRY

Did you ride the Greyhound?

ALAN

Yeah.

JERRY

You know, I like you!

(*Hugs him enthusiastically.*)

I didn't know if I would or not, but you're nice. How come you didn't come to live with us a long time ago?

ALAN

You don't remember visiting me and the zoo? In Omaha?

JERRY

No. Mom's told me, though. It seems weird having a new brother and already he's as big as Dad. You should have been living with us when we had the farm.

ALAN

Did you have a farm?

JERRY

Your head still hurt?

ALAN

Yeah.

JERRY

(*After a pause.*)

Jack and me called it a farm, but we just had a big open lot
with a bunch of trees.

ALAN

An orchard?

JERRY

Kinda—we had some orange trees and a plum tree and a fig
tree——

ALAN

You had orange trees?

JERRY

Oh, sure.

ALAN

I've never seen them growing before.

JERRY

We used to have oranges all the time. Me and Jack used to make
orangeade and sell it, only nobody ever bought it, because they
had more oranges than we did. Dad bought it and we drank it.

ALAN

(*After a pause.*)

Oh, God. I like you, too.

(*Squeezes him. To the audience.*)

So I didn't sleep, I guess. Not much, that first night. And the
last thing I wanted to do, or thought of doing——

DOUGLAS

(*Entering.*)

We'll just drive in, you make your application—it'll take about
ten minutes' time—and we can drive over and take a peek at the
ocean you haven't seen.

43

ALAN

(*To the audience and them, following Douglas into the kitchen for coffee.*)

The personnel manager at Ryan Aeronautical hated me on sight, with no love lost.

DOUGLAS

Aw, that son of a bitch, all that brass—ball-breaking office flunkies. That's all they are, Alan; ignore him, don't give him the time of day.

ALAN

Do we have to go today? I can hardly see.

DOUGLAS

He's going on a month's vacation tomorrow. They can process you while he's gone. You won't start working for a month.

CAROL

Buy now, pay later.

ALAN

Maybe I should do something else: grocery clerk or something.

DOUGLAS

Well, what do you want, boy? It's up to you. Do you want to make enough to go to school or do you want to go to the movies? We'll all go; we'll go on to the beach later.

ALAN

No, it didn't take long. He said we have two divisions of engineering personnel: temporary and full-time. I said I would much prefer the former, and he said there was a greater possibility of being hired in the *latter*, and that was that. So, providing I'm not lying about never having joined the Communist party or something, I'll be set. I'll start in a month or so.

DOUGLAS

As soon as he's back.

ALAN

At the Aeronautical Engineering Training Center riveting school.

44

PENNY

How can you manage full-time work and full-time school?

DOUGLAS

So he'll go part time to school until he can get on temporary at the plant.

ALAN

No, no.

DOUGLAS

Well, I say if you can cut both full time, why not? Now, if you're serious about working down there, they have a scholarship program. You can go into electrodynamics or something like that, and they'll pay the bill, all the way——

ALAN

It's my second term; I don't know what I want yet.

DOUGLAS

Well, don't be negative; give it a fair shake. Just objectively, what's happening in the world—they're putting rockets into space; they got hydrogen bombs and cobalt bombs, atomic submarines; they bounce signals off Mars and Venus and every other goddamned thing.

ALAN

I know.

DOUGLAS

Physicists are looking at the sunspots and predicting the weather. Every field. All of them, what you need——

ALAN

I don't know anything——

DOUGLAS

——is physics, by God.

CAROL

That sounds like a good book.

(*Alan laughs.*)

DOUGLAS

Well, you can joke around—I just want you to think about it. All I'm saying is, if I was a kid now, it wouldn't take me three

45

minutes—three seconds—to make up my mind. Engineering, electrodynamics; you just have to open your eyes.

ALAN

And of course the head is worse—But the ocean! I've lived eight hundred miles from it all my life!

RONNIE

(Coming into the kitchen with Jack.)

I wish you would, but only if you want to.

ALAN

No, I like you very—

(To the audience.)

I'm embarrassed and I've no idea how to tell her.

(To Ronnie.)

I'll call you Ronnie, like Dad does; I couldn't! I like you very much! You know!

(Grabbing Jack and wooling his hair.)

And you! Brush ape! Nut! Huh? This is the other one. Jack. Can you see his arms? He's covered all over with white hair. He's our little white orangutan. He's had straight A's since the day he was born.

JACK

Yes.

ALAN

And he's a smart ass—I mean aleck.

JACK

Yes.

ALAN

Yes.

JACK

What's an aleck?

ALAN

I don't know, but you're one.

(To the audience.)

Don't you wish you had a smart answer for all those simple-minded great questions he asks? Like, an aleck is a something or other without its watchicallit, and you're going to be one if you

46

keep asking—Oh, Jack! Jack Jack. He's so bright the teachers think it's unhealthy. Go go go go.
(*Jack and Jerry go, running off.*)
I won't! I promise I won't!
(*To Ronnie.*)
And you can't either——

RONNIE

O.K., O.K., I won't——

ALAN

I won't tell you a lot of juvenile anecdotes, but I want—I want to bronze the little bastards and sit them up on the mantelpiece. One! Just one I'll tell while they're gone, one quick one. I want to get badly, badly drunk and distribute a walletful of slobbered-on and bent-up photographs all along the bar and say, notice his hair, notice that one's toes, look at those teeth. Just one little anecdote that Ronnie told me. When Jerry was five, they all went up in an airplane—big thrill for Jerry, who used to watch airplanes take off by the hour when they lived by the airport. So they're all in the plane. Jerry's on Ronnie's lap, and after they've been off the ground for a few minutes, he squirms around and whispers excitedly in Ronnie's ear: "When do we start getting small?"

DOUGLAS

(*In the darkroom. Red light on. Projector light on.*)
That's *on* now. Two three four five.
(*Projector off.*)

ALAN

(*Walking to the darkroom.*)
How can you tell when to turn it off?

DOUGLAS

You have to know what you want. The less you expose it, the lighter it is; the more you expose it, the darker. You burn it in.

ALAN

When did you take this?

DOUGLAS

Couple a months ago.

ALAN

And you're just now getting around to printing them?

DOUGLAS

Aw, I got no time. Wow! Look at that! I tell you, boy, mmmm. Don't crowd, now; just don't crowd.

(*Alan laughs.*)

Is she a piece? Huh? Look at those boobs. Hummf. I tell you.

ALAN

She isn't the least bit overdoing it, you don't think?

DOUGLAS

What do you talk, with a butt like that?

ALAN

That's what I was looking at.

DOUGLAS

Can't miss that, huh? That's too broad for you? Hell, you got a lot to get a hold on there. Oh, yeah.

RONNIE

(*To the audience as the lights brighten.*)

Well, Mrs. Collins said she wouldn't let her husband out to take pictures of bare-assed girls in the woods over her dead body, and I made the mistake of saying it kept Doug off the streets.

CAROL

(*To Alan.*)

So she hasn't spoken to Ronnie since.

RONNIE

Really. Well, how was I to know her husband spent half his time on Delmarco Street?

ALAN

I take it that's the——

CAROL

Right.

ALAN

And now she's not speaking to you.

(*Half to the audience, then fully.*)

San Diego is just like all other towns just under seven hundred thousand. And California. Californians. They're insane. Well, you've seen the movies they make out here; they have no idea at all what people are like. Well, it's not their fault; they've got nothing to go on—they're working in the dark. They're mad. They are. The shoes they wear, when they wear shoes; the clothes they wear, when they wear clothes. This place is impossible. Nobody walks. Nobody walks. Anywhere. Two blocks —if the old man has the car you don't go. You drive to a movie and they're all drive-ins. The food is all drive-ins—mini-hamburgers and cherry malts. The traffic is seventy miles an hour bumper-to-bumper going into town, six lanes abreast. The supermarkets. They're mad. They take up blocks. They're open twenty-four hours and they're packed jammed full with— Four in the morning, they're buying watermelon and lettuce and a ham and a gallon of Gallo port, and they've got the kids and the babies and the shopping cart and the portable radio and the whole family—the sandals flopping. They're nuts! They live on the beach. They all cook outside and eat outside and sleep outside—and of course it's a beautiful outside to do it in. Downtown San Diego is white day and night with sailors and those big fluffy moths and sea gulls and pigeons and sand, and I've finally seen the ocean. All of us, we had to beg Dad to take a picture of us. He's not taken a picture of the kids, Ronnie said, in almost two years.

RONNIE

He's got a hundred tons of cheesecake.

ALAN

All lined up, the three of us.

RONNIE

Doug's mother wrote today and said that that wasn't Alan, that was Doug when he was seventeen.

DOUGLAS

I told you! What'd I say!

RONNIE

That was Douglas when he was seventeen.

DOUGLAS

I said it was! By God! You can't—no matter what anybody

anywhere says! . . . Wait till we get you flying by in a flashy MG. I tell you, sir-ee-bob!

ALAN

MG?

DOUGLAS

Or Porche or Austin, one of those babies.

ALAN

Blue.

DOUGLAS

Red, hell, red. Man, what do you talk?

ALAN

Purple. Compromise.

DOUGLAS

Huh?

(*Ronnie and Alan laugh.*)

ALAN

It's beautiful. It is. I always wanted a big old family like this; it's just great. And it's not going to last. . . .

CAROL

(*Holding a bottle of pills, takes one with a glass of water.*) Well, that ought to take the hair off!

ALAN

(*To the audience.*)

Of course we're immediately in a conspiracy.

PENNY

What are they—dope?

CAROL

Oh, yell it out, Penny, and get us all kicked outta here—dope. Good God. You know that paint that little boys spray on little model airplanes?

PENNY

Yes. O.K., I know.

CAROL

Smells like ether; it could kill you if you breathe too deeply?

PENNY

I said Yes——

CAROL

Well, that's dope. Dope.

(*Beat.*)

They're a very innocent sounding p-i-l-l called Mellaril. One of
the seven wonder drugs, and you're going to ask what it does;
well, it does wonders.

PENNY

Are they strong?

CAROL

They're stronger than I am.

(*Messing with Alan's hair.*)

What do you think, Douglas?

PENNY

It's called a duck's tail.

DOUGLAS

What you want a duck's ass on the back of your head?

(*With humor.*)

You want it all swirled around like that, you look like—I don't
know what—like some of those high-school punks or Penny's
whatsit.

CAROL

You don't like it? Doug, you're square; you can't get around it.

DOUGLAS

What the hell are you talking? He looks like a drugstore
cowboy.

CAROL

Doug, you don't know your ass.

DOUGLAS

(*Too sharply.*)

Who you telling about ass?

PENNY

Phil even wears his hair like——

DOUGLAS

(*Enormous.*)

Miss Innocence, we just won't talk about the way your boyfriends . . . do anything, huh? *Huh?*

ALAN

(*A long embarrassed pause; then quickly.*)

Dad combs his hair straight back and has since the day he was born, and that's the only way to comb your hair. It's been just twenty-four hours. And the head's still beating and it's all too fast. In six months I'll be sleeping in a park in Chicago with a letter in my pocket from Ronnie telling me that Carol is dead. But who would know that now? We're sitting down to eat. Outside. That's California. We're——

CAROL

Shhhhh!

(*He stops. They listen a split second.*)

No, not thunder; you feel it?

ALAN

No. Yes! I think——

CAROL

Shhhhh!

(*They concentrate.*)

ALAN

Yeah. Good God.

RONNIE

You get used to it. It doesn't bother the natives. If it *thunders*, they run out into the street and think the world's coming to an end.

ALAN

They don't have thunderstorms out here?

RONNIE

Almost never. I've heard it thunder maybe four times in twelve years. People nearly died of heart attack; it even scared me the last time.

ALAN

Could I have another coffee?

RONNIE

Shhhhh!

ALAN

(*Smiling at it, aside to the audience.*)

It feels like—you've felt it in the cities—when a big loaded, lumbering diesel rolls by outside; or if you live near a subway and the whole building—all the walls, the chair you're sitting in —gives a gentle, prolonged shudder. That's it. Only there's no truck going by—it just happens of its own accord.

PENNY

Shhhhh!

RONNIE

There, feel it!

(*A beat as they listen between all these lines.*)

ALAN

(*Smiling.*)

Good God.

DOUGLAS

See? Isn't that sumpin?

JACK

It's silly.

PENNY

Did you hear?

CAROL

Shhhhh!

(*They all concentrate, smiling, feeling the vibrations.*)

RONNIE

(*Very gently, slowly, to them. No one changes his position.*)

Feel it?

(*They continue to smile, tensed, intently concentrating. Five seconds or just over.*)

(*Slow curtain.*)

INTERMISSION.

Act Two

(Alan, Penny, and Carol outside. Bright sunlight. Carol is in a vivid orange robe over a bathing suit.)

ALAN

(To the audience.)

Same song, second verse, as the poet said; couldn't be better but it's gonna be worse. March. April. May. June or July or August. About. Everything goes well enough, but it's complicated. It's difficult to leave well enough alone.

CAROL

Because "well enough" is an intolerable state to be in. Take it from me.

ALAN

I'm home today for a—home. Oh, wow. And it is now. Really is. For a short time. A very short time longer. My last class is at three usually, and I go to work from school. Today is Saturday —no school, work, no school—so I can spend some time home before we leave for work at five. Penny and Carol are on vacation. . . . It's summer.

PENNY

I still don't know why you started school summer term.

ALAN

Because I was very suspicious that if I didn't, I wouldn't start at all. Two momentous events have elapsed! Dad has developed an absolute passion for milk. And he's teaching Penny photography.

PENNY

Well, not photography. There isn't anything to learn except point and snap. I'm learning developing and printing.

ALAN

You like it?

PENNY

Sure, it's fascinating. I'm a little sick of seeing that red, white, and blue bikini in every picture we print.

CAROL

Ha!

ALAN

Dad's got this bikini he takes along to his sessions with the girls——

CAROL

It's pathetic.

ALAN

——and the whole session is taken up, apparently—we only see the pictures—with first coaxing her into it and then nearly out of it. She unties it here and pushes it down there—or else she doesn't. Which is even funnier.

PENNY

It's awful. It's cotton and tacky and just ugly as it can be.

ALAN

(*To Carol.*)

I'm surprised he hasn't got you posing for him by now.

CAROL

Oh, honey, I'm onto that crap. He squires around those dames down to the beach with that stupid car——

ALAN

Chrysler convertible.

CAROL

Nothing but big cars in this play——

ALAN

Right, which isn't typical—some of the guys build their own, so they drive these sorta car-collages.

CAROL

But Doug squeals around in this big fat Chrysler, which is perfect, but he doesn't know it. He took a million pictures of me; I'm not photogenic—he didn't even notice it. It's all in his head —he never notices. Slobbering around: "You got nice eyes," "You got nice legs," "You got nice tits." Hell, I haven't even *got* tits, the creep.

ALAN

Probably he wanted you to——

CAROL

He wanted in my pants. It was humiliating. When a girl seventeen has to tell a man forty-five to grow up, something's wrong. I just found it repellent and I told him.

ALAN

Not in those words, I hope.

CAROL

Yes, in those words: "Doug, grow up; you're repellent." Listen, half the foster fathers I've had have tried to make me. Since I was six. It's not my scene. Men are asses. If they knew what they looked like, they'd all march into the sea in a line, like lemmicks.

PENNY

It isn't lemmicks; it's lemmings.

CAROL

You're terrific. I think you're my favorite sister.
(*To Alan, who laughs.*)
You can go to hell, too.

ALAN

I went to one outing with Dad, and whatever you do, you have got—you have *got*—to go to an amateur photographers' meeting with cheesecake models. We went up to Redwood—out in this cactus park with about four hundred photographers and about forty girls. Ten to one. And they're draping over every fence and adobe wall and bench in the park. I've got this thirty-five millimeter Leica that Dad's lent me, barely explaining how to work the damn thing. And all the guys are frisking around this gal—she's on a Mexican serape—and the guys are practically having heart attacks: Clickadyclickadyclickadyclickady-clickady all around like a plague of locusts, and they're all jockeying for the best angle to shoot straight down her breasts, which are pumpkins; and they're giving her: "That's it, honey. Wet your lips, baby. Wet 'em again. Give us a laugh. Now slack. Slack. Just let everything go to hell. Toss your hair. Pout. Pout. Indignant. Hate. More. Hate. Kill. Kill. . . . Thatagirl. Wet your lips, keep 'em wet—not so uch. Pout. Just let it all hang——"

CAROL

That's insane.

ALAN

"Just give us a big sexy kiss!" And I'm standing there with this damn dumb Leica, saying, "Oh, I don't know, could you just sorta, maybe—smile?"

CAROL

I know that whole scene.

DOUGLAS

(*Entering.*)

Hey, Alan, how come you didn't show?

ALAN

Huh? Where?

DOUGLAS

This guy is impossible, isn't he? Where? I mean this wasn't important, but he'd forget it if it was.

(*Giving Alan's head a wrench.*)

Is your head on tight? We wouldn't want you losing that.

ALAN

Yeah, yeah, I think. What did I forget?

DOUGLAS

Club meeting yesterday afternoon. Nothing happened. You can go to them or not; suit yourself.

ALAN

(*To the audience.*)

The few times I have gone, you couldn't——

DOUGLAS

(*Interrupting. Serious afterthought.*)

Al—hey!

ALAN

Huh?

DOUGLAS

Stanley tells me you're not coming to work. Something like three days last week you missed? Awhile back? What was that?

ALAN

Three days? No. Maybe two once, but not three.

DOUGLAS

What the hell's so important? The days I don't drive you in,
you're just not showing up? I have to squire you in?

ALAN

I have been.

DOUGLAS

He says you're a good worker—
(*Half to the audience.*)
—He's a good worker; he picks things up—but you can't——

ALAN

Listen, I still do more in three days than the other guys——

DOUGLAS

They're getting their five days' pay, and you're——

ALAN

You should watch the shop steward sometime. Oh, wow. I
thought your department sat around on their retired duffs.
There were guys——

DOUGLAS

Retired duffs?
(*Mock indignation.*)
I'll have you know—I mean a few Government Jobs that's very
important stuff——

ALAN

Right, right.
(*To the audience.*)
"Government Jobs" is slang for doing something of your own.
(*Back to Douglas.*)
I went in the other day and two different guys were making
mailboxes, and one guy was repairing his wife's Mixmaster.

DOUGLAS

Well, they're paying you to come to work five days a week,
man; that's what——

ALAN

They're paying me by the hour. Maybe one week I missed two
days because of tests at school I had to cram——

61

DOUGLAS

Well, learn to study—crap—organize yourself, man. You take
a job, you go; it's a simple thing.

ALAN

Dad spoke for me down there, and he thinks I'm giving him a
bad name taking off—I'm a beatnik.

DOUGLAS

They want you there five days a week. They don't give a damn
if you sit on your fanny or stand on your head, man; they don't
care as long as you show up.

ALAN

You know, that's true; they really don't. You should see those
guys—nobody works. Nobody works. It's amazing!
(*Including the audience.*)
I could tell you the name of the transportation jets we're building
down there and how we're doing it—the entire aircraft industry
would collapse tomorrow morning. Would you believe chewing
gum? I'm not kidding. There's a little hole, no one's looking,
what the hell! I don't miss that much, really.

DOUGLAS

You just see that you get whatever it is you have to do done
today so we can leave on time. I'm not going to wait around
for you. . . .

ALAN

(*To the audience.*)
So what do you do when you hear that? You decide right there
that you're not going, right?

DOUGLAS

(*Instantly furious.*)
You think it's funny—you want to do it now? Huh?

ALAN

Later.

DOUGLAS

You want to do it now? We'll do it now. Come on, we'll do it
now.

62

ALAN

We'll get to it. Later.

DOUGLAS

(*Looks at him a moment, then to Penny casually.*)
Penny, we're gonna work right after lunch, O.K.?

PENNY

Whenever.

(*Douglas exits.*)
I keep asking him to print up some of his pictures of Grand
Canyon or something, but it's always those darn girls—girls are
so stupid to do that. Oh, I guess they think of a career, but,
wow, that's so stupid. It's no worse than me, though; I'm always
imagining my wedding. Do you do that?

CAROL

Do what?

PENNY

I can't pass a church some days without going through my
whole wedding in it. You know, I'm running out of the door
in my wedding dress with my hands over my head, keeping off
the rice and trying to wave to everybody at the same time.
Sometimes I'm sitting perfectly still and I catch myself tossing
my bouquet at someone.

CAROL

Who are you thinking about marrying?

PENNY

Well . . . I'm not. I don't want to get married. I'd like to be a
scientist just as much. I picture that too.

CAROL

Penny has a very rich fantasy life.

PENNY

Well, I do. I think it's healthy. I see myself in one of those white
lab coats with a bunch of those bubbly test tubes and coils all
around—analyzing blood and making notations——

CAROL

Blood? Good God, you have the most morbid goddamn sense of
duty.

PENNY

Do you like being away from Sonny as much as being with him?

CAROL

What?

PENNY

Really, it's funny, but I think sometimes when I'm with Phil I'd really rather not be, so I could be away from him—*wanting* to be with him. You like Phil, don't you? He's nice, isn't he?

CAROL

Do I? I don't know him.

PENNY

You went to school with him before he graduated; I didn't. I'll bet he was popular at Grossmont, wasn't he?

CAROL

(*Spiritedly.*)

I didn't know him. We didn't run in the same crowd. I thought he was a stuck-up jerk. He's all right. He's nice. He's beautiful. Yes, he was popular. My God, I guess he was. Aren't there any boys at your school?

PENNY

I don't go with any of them——

ALAN

(*Overlapping some.*)

Carol goes to Grossmont; Penny goes to El Cajon.

PENNY

My gosh, why don't you like Phil? Good grief. All we can ever talk about is Sonny. . . . I don't even like Texas. I don't know what a Hereford looks like. I'll bet you don't, either.

(*To Alan.*)

She used to talk about all of Sonny's beautiful Black Anguses. She didn't know if they were horses or automobiles.

(*Beat. To Carol.*)

Are you going to marry Sonny?

CAROL

I hope to hell. I'm not going to come this far at such unimaginable expense and wind up—and I'm going to invite all my scores and wear white. I can't wait.

(*Digging in her purse.*)

Goddammit! I brought a bottle of baby oil, out here—I'll bet I spend a fortune just from losing—

(*Penny hands her the bottle of oil from beside the chair.*)

Penny, why don't you put on your swimsuit? You're going to just bake.

PENNY

No, I'm not staying.

CAROL

Well, you're driving me nuts out here dressed up like an Eskimo.

(*To Alan, handing him the oil.*)

Get my back, will you?

ALAN

You don't need that stuff.

CAROL

I have delicate skin.

ALAN

What is that you put over your eyes? Plastic spoons? You know, I knew a girl once who went blind from sunbathing with plastic spoons over her eyes. They melted. You're going to be solid brown with white eyelids.

CAROL

Would you shut up?

ALAN

(*To the audience as he rubs Carol's back.*)

Ronnie, about a month ago—I came in moaning that I was failing what? Math, probably—I'm failing math every other day. And she said, "The term isn't over yet; you've got to have faith." You have to understand she was serious as hell about it. It scared us to death. I really believed it. She said, "If you have faith the size of a mustard seed, you——"

CAROL

Turn it down, why don't you?

ALAN

(*Stops rubbing her back.*)

I'm going to stop because I think you're enjoying this in all the wrong ways.

(*To the audience.*)

You have to understand I thought I'd probably exposed myself to trichinosis.

CAROL

You went in and washed your hands.

ALAN

I did not. How many pills today?

CAROL

Who counts any more? Three or four so far, and that's pretty far.

PENNY

You shouldn't take those and lie in the sun.

CAROL

God, the things you're opposed to. You're worse than Sonny sometimes.

PENNY

I'm not opposed to them; you just shouldn't. Maybe I should go with Sonny and you go with Phil.

CAROL

(*Rapidly strung together.*)

That does it! I'm going to take a shower. Penny, do you have any bobby pins something has to happen to—don't answer; you don't use them, right? What kind of sister are you anyway? I swear to God. You don't know *any* two-part harmony songs. You don't buy cheap perfumes I can steal, you don't use a brush, you're immoral—always suggesting we swap husbands. What the hell good are you outside of making peanut butter divinity? Jesus H. Christopher, I wish I were on the moon. I nearly am.

PENNY

Well, why do you take them? You know Ronnie will kick you out if she finds out and Sonny made it a condition.

ALAN

He didn't make it a condition; he just said he'd never speak to her again.

CAROL

It turns me off. It turns me way, way off.

ALAN

It's a kind of Norwegian Fly.

CAROL

Icelandic.

ALAN

(*Singing.*)

"Try Icelandic Fly, gets you there on time . . ."

CAROL

You couldn't possibly have said that; that song didn't come out for ages.

ALAN

That's all right; you aren't even alive. You've been dead ten years.

(*They laugh.*)

CAROL

I would like to thank the theatre for rescuing me from that dreary cupboard in that dreary condition.

PENNY

Dank.

ALAN

Drear.

CAROL

(*Overlapping them.*)

I want to—right—thank the drear management for the magic of the theatre, which enables me to be continually young and alive and beautiful and current——

PENNY

And here.

ALAN

Topical.

PENNY

God, yes, topical.

ALAN

We hope.

CAROL

(*Biting her lip, sitting down, almost in tears.*)
Shit.

ALAN

Hey, Carol, come on, it's all right.

CAROL

A lot you know, buddy, a lot you know.

ALAN

Really—remember those Red Skelton radio programs, and he
played the mean widdle kid?

PENNY

Yeah, right——

ALAN

He used to describe something dreadful that happened to
him and start crying, "I scared me widdle self"?

CAROL

I don't remember.

ALAN

I think you scared you widdle self.

PENNY

Sure you remember. On the radio. I remember it.

ALAN

Maybe she listened to a different program: Fibber and Molly
McGee.
(*Beat.*)
Don't get maudlin, Carol.

CAROL

I'm not only locked in your goddamned sideshow, dragged out
to play second fiddle in a three-ring—
(*Slinging a cigarette all the way off, out the wings; walking
away a few steps, furious.*)
Fuck!

ALAN
(*Calling.*)
Come on, come off it, munghead.

PENNY
Mung? Wow.

CAROL
I hope it burns down the theatre.

PENNY
That's the worst kind of head, munghead.

CAROL
I'm hip.
(*After a deep breath she regains composure, waves it away.*)
O.K., I'm back.

ALAN
She's back.
(*Singing.*)
She's back and she's better than ever before, Campbell's Pork
and Beans.

ALAN and PENNY and CAROL
(*Three-part harmony. Quite on the patio, not for the audience.*)
>   Back and they're better than ever before,
>   Back and they're better than ever before,
>   Back and they're better than ever before,
>   Campbell's Pork and Beans. Hey!

(*Jerry and Jack come running in.*)

ALAN
(*To the audience immediately.*)
Most of the radio stations out here are incredible. They're three
times as powerful as allowed by the FCC or whoever, but the
broadcasting towers are all in Mexico, so they can get away with
anything. They play rock 'n' roll all day and night, and commercials, commercials—more than you'd ever believe—and
about half of them are in Spanish, so—
(*To Jerry.*)
Come on. So they go like this:

69

JERRY

Para refrescarse tome Coca-Cola *frío.*

ALAN

Isn't that great? Well, what's that got to do with the story? Well . . . nothing, actually; only we feel we should throw in a little local color from time to time.

CAROL

(*Announcement.*)

Local Color!

PENNY

It takes awhile for the untutored eye to recognize it, but——

CAROL

——the color green does not occur in California naturally.

ALAN

(*To the audience.*)

Southern California is in the colors of perpetually early autumn: umber, amber, olive, sienna, ocher, orange; acres and acres of mustard and sage—the colors.

PENNY

(*Straight.*)

The herbs, too.

ALAN

And grass dies. It has a season of winter and the weather does not. So instead of grass they plant—a lot of the lawns are planted in dichondra. A little cloverlike thing that grows about two inches high and doesn't require mowing, and it's very cute; but it isn't grass, is it? And it's green the year round.

CAROL

Only not green.

ALAN

Right. And that bright eye-breaking, bright-sun-shining-through-oak-and-maple-and-elm-onto-bright-green-ferns-and-grass green does not occur. Of course, you couldn't care less. It's something you rather gladly or at least unknowingly forfeit for nearly continual sunshine.

PENNY

Weren't we doing a play awhile back?

ALAN
Right!
(*Everyone listening to Ronnie, who has entered during the last sentence. Ronnie in mid-sentence. Another time, earlier.*)

RONNIE
. . . the size of a mustard seed, you can move mountains.

PENNY
Can you work math?

ALAN
Well, I don't seem——

RONNIE
(*Very seriously—mock religiously.*)
No, now, I'm not kidding. The Bible says you can move mountains, and you can. And I have that faith.

PENNY
And you can move mountains?

RONNIE
It doesn't matter what you three feel, it's my faith that's important. Now, do you see Mount Helix out there?

ALAN
(*As they look.*)
Are you kidding?

PENNY
Come on——

RONNIE
No, now, we're all going to look away. Go on——

PENNY
That's sacri——

RONNIE
——look away now; it's a simple demonstration of my faith.
(*They turn away from the mountain.*)

ALAN
Right. Now what?

RONNIE
Now. When we turn around again, Mount Helix will be gone. Because I have that faith. Because I know it will be gone. In my

heart. Now turn around slowly, and Mount Helix will be gone. Now.

ALAN

You.

(*They don't believe, but they are a little uncertain.*)

RONNIE

(*Turns slowly and gazes off.*)

Well . . .

CAROL

What?

RONNIE

Just like I thought, there it is. Damn.

ALAN

What?

PENNY

Don't scare me.

(*They laugh.*)

RONNIE

I must have miscalculated. Look at it.

CAROL

Yeah, I think so.

RONNIE

I think it's even grown. My faith isn't the size of a mustard seed, it's the size of a poppy seed. And poppy seed don't move nothing.

CAROL

Poppy seed moves the world.

RONNIE

That's a different poppy seed.

CAROL

(*In starting to get up, drops the bottle of pills, picks it up, nearly falls over. Holding her head and trying to put the bottle into a pocket of the robe.*)

Oh, wow.

RONNIE

Are you O.K.? You look like hell.

CAROL

(*Nearly floating away, trying to come down a little.*)

Hmmm? I'm sorry, I washed my brain and I can't do a thing
with it. Where are you?

(*She gets the bottle into the pocket, will not look at Ronnie
directly.*)

RONNIE

What's wrong? Look at me.

CAROL

(*Handling the robe to Penny.*)

Penny, sweetheart, could you take this in?

RONNIE

What's wrong?

(*Penny takes the robe in.*)

CAROL

No, I'm O.K. I ate something; it didn't agree with me.

RONNIE

Look up. Is that all?

CAROL

Well, it's my *time,* as the Victorians would have it. I'm dizzy
a little is all.

(*She exits. Penny has taken the robe away and is back now.
Ronnie looks at Alan and Penny a moment. Some tension.*)

RONNIE

(*Rather to the audience, breaking away.*)

Well, once in awhile you have to admit you don't understand
a thing about what kids are doing with their lives nowadays.

(*All the others enter for lunch.*)

PENNY

. . . because they went all the way to the top of Mount Helix
and dragged down this poor palm tree.

RONNIE

I told you it wouldn't grow.

ALAN

Well, how would Jerry and I know that? This poor baby palm
was thriving in the garbage heap; we transplanted it into the

73

back yard, next to Jack's bird of paradise, and the poor little palm died before sundown. With its boots on.

CAROL

Boots off, I think.

ALAN

Well, whichever is the nobler.

RONNIE

I think it's two separate schools of thought.

JERRY

Off! "I ain't gonna die, partner, with those damn boots on!"

DOUGLAS

Jerry, don't say "damn" in front of your brother; he won't be old enough to say that for fifteen years yet.

JERRY

Why not?

RONNIE

And you've got a few years to go yourself.

JERRY

What should I say?

JACK

Say "hockey."

DOUGLAS

That's enough out of you, too—no hints from the gallery, peanut.

CAROL

He's a lady-killer.

JERRY

What can I say if I can't say that?

CAROL

How racy should it be?

JERRY

Pretty racy.

CAROL

Well, you should try——

JACK

"Hanged."

JERRY

Yes! That hanged thing ain't worth the powder it'd take to blow it——

RONNIE

No, no.

JACK

Danged. Danged.

JERRY

All-fired.

RONNIE

No. Say . . . I can't think of one. Well, don't use any of them —good grief, there's at least——

JACK

Good grief!

RONNIE

No, don't say "good grief" either. There're two hundred thousand acceptable words in the language; you don't have to wallow around in the vernacular at your age.

JERRY

I don't know two hundred thousand——

DOUGLAS

Well, you better be for learning them.

JERRY

How do I know if they're acceptable?

RONNIE

O.K. You come to me and whisper them in my ear, and if they happen not to be acceptable, I'll wash your mouth out with soap.

JERRY

No.

RONNIE

See? I thought not.
(*They are leaving.*)
What do you say?

JACK

May we be excused?

RONNIE

Yes, you may; don't tear the house down.

(*Jack and Jerry exit.*)

The kids on the block have a bucket brigade of profanity. I think they have a collective mind. One of them learns a new word and everyone on the block knows it in an hour. We had an entire month of "shitfire" last year. I can't imagine where they got that one, but they loved it.

CAROL

Probably from Douglas.

RONNIE

(*To Carol.*)

You aren't supposed to say that.

DOUGLAS

They aren't supposed to listen. Hell, I wouldn't want them to be like Alan's college buddies up at State: all potatoes and no meat. They all look like they're made out of unbaked dough. They even talk like it.

ALAN

My friends? Whatta you talk? My friends swear like sailors; it's part of the emancipated-young-adult jargon.

DOUGLAS

Well, I'd be surprised if they knew what it meant. We dropped him off the other morning——

ALAN

Yeah, yeah, last month sometime you dropped me off.

DOUGLAS

Two weeks ago Friday.

ALAN

Compromise purple.

(*To the audience; aside.*)

Now, you see, I think that's the funniest line in the play.

DOUGLAS

And he introduced Ronnie and me to a few of them. Sasha and Joan and Owen and—don't they ever get out into the sun?

76

ALAN

Into the sun? Are you kidding? Oh, my God—into the sun! I've discovered there's this whole beautiful poetical intellectual coterie that wouldn't be caught dead in the sun. They're nuts, but they're great. Kinda like the Castilian Spanish: the whiter you are, the brighter you are. They're nuts, but you love them for it. A lot of the young kids out at State——

DOUGLAS

Young? Young? Young? Them? Oh, man, they're on their pensions. Who are you trying to kid? They're cadavers. Ronnie, you read—Carol, did you see that magazine thing they put out at State?

CAROL

No.

ALAN

I brought that home: I haven't even seen it yet——

DOUGLAS

(Overlapping.)

Well, that's what I'm talking, Ronnie. Right there. I want you to look at it some night and see if it can turn you on.

CAROL

What he's saying, Alan, is it doesn't stack up to the garage collection of the complete Erle Stanley Gardner——

DOUGLAS

Listen, twit, unless you've read those books, just don't knock them. People are a darn sight more interested in life than in those plants and those creepy ferns and creepy shadows and creepy creeps. Nobody reads that magazine except your creepy college would-be poets. Oh, man, I didn't graduate from high school, and I'll bet I can take any of them on in anything except arithmetic, huh?

ALAN

Dad and I are both rotten with figures.

DOUGLAS

Some kinds of figures.

ALAN

Probably you could.

DOUGLAS

Yeah, you damn-betcha. What do they retain? Huh? History: I'll bet you don't even know the Presidents of the country. Your own goddamned country. Do you?

ALAN

God, no. I only know the capitals of the states because I had a jigsaw puzzle.

DOUGLAS

And the vice-presidents.

ALAN

I don't know any of the vice-presidents except Truman.

DOUGLAS

Well, I don't imagine ten out of the eight thousand of them know them either. Who was Washington's vice-president?

ALAN

I don't know.

DOUGLAS

The first vice-president of the United States?

ALAN

I said no. I'm stupid.

PENNY

Adams.

DOUGLAS

Right.

PENNY

Only, that's it.

DOUGLAS

(*Reciting rhythmically.*)

Washington—Adams; Adams—Jefferson; Jefferson—Burr; Jefferson—Clinton; Madison—Clinton; Madison—Gerry; Monroe—Tompkins; Adams—Calhoun; Jackson—Calhoun; Jackson—Van Buren; Van Buren—Johnson; Harrison—*Tyler!*

ALAN

Hey, that's great. And many more, huh? Tyler of "Tippecanoe and Tyler Too" fame?

DOUGLAS

Right. . . .

ALAN

Who was Teddy Roosevelt's first vice-president?

DOUGLAS

(*Beat.*)

Cleveland—Stevenson; McKinley—Hobart; McKinley—Roosevelt; Roosevelt and nobody; Roosevelt—*Fairbanks*.

(*Beat; then building.*)

Taft—Sherman; Wilson—Marshall; Harding—Coolidge; Coolidge—Dawes; Hoover—Curtis; Roosevelt—Garner; Roosevelt—Wallace; Roosevelt—*Truman!*

(*A very long pause. Silence. Everyone is still.*)

JERRY

(*Entering with a small postage-stamp-sized piece of photograph.*)

Look at me; that's terrible. Right across my ear.

RONNIE

What?

JERRY

My picture. The picture Dad took of us.

RONNIE

Doug, you didn't tear that up, did you?

DOUGLAS

What? Tear what up?

ALAN

I wanted a print of that.

DOUGLAS

What? It isn't any good.

RONNIE

Your mother loved it; I told you what she said.

DOUGLAS

Well, Mother, bless her heart, doesn't know much about photography.

ALAN

Well, I don't either, but I wanted one.

DOUGLAS

No, I tore it up; it was a bad print anyway; it's too light. I'll
print it up again.

ALAN

You never even intended to.

DOUGLAS

(*Quite directly.*)

Well, now, how do you know what I intended to do and what
the hell I didn't intend to do? Huh?

RONNIE

It's the only picture we had of them; you haven't taken a picture of the boys in two years.

DOUGLAS

It was a lousy picture—I'll take another one—the light was
bad. It was a snapshot, for God's sake. Penny, are you going to
help me or not, huh?

PENNY

Yeah, I will.

JERRY

He tore it right across my ear.

ALAN

I really wanted it.

DOUGLAS

(*Much too loud for the occasion.*)

All right, now, will you just shut up about the goddamned
picture now! Now I've *had it! With you!*

(*He exits with Penny.*)

RONNIE

(*Topically.*)

Doug and I had a terrible argument about you last night.

ALAN

What? Wait a sec—I'm not getting the drift of——

RONNIE

(*Going on.*)

Actually, he argued. He said—you should excuse the expression
—you hadn't had a piece of ass since you'd been here.

ALAN

I hadn't what?

DOUGLAS

(*To Ronnie as the two are suddenly isolated in the living room.*)
You saw that gang of dough-balls he was hanging out with at
school.

RONNIE

I don't know if he's quite "hanging out" with them.

DOUGLAS

Well, I'm not saying *what* he's doing with them; I know what
he's not doing. When has he been on a date? Squiring Cookie to
the local movie in El Cajon and back twice, what's that supposed to mean?

RONNIE

Well, you could hardly expect him to go for Cookie; Cookie's
hardly the freshest thing on the block—and it's a small block.

DOUGLAS

When's he gone out?

RONNIE

I don't know; when's he had time? Full-time work, full-time
school.

DOUGLAS

Oh, time's ass. Summer term, everyone else on vacation; goddammit, he hangs around the house, he hangs around school.
He hasn't had a piece of ass since he's been here.

RONNIE

Well, he's been here four or five months. I don't know.

DOUGLAS

Well nothing! He's not getting anything from that gang of

dishwater dames at school, and if he is, he ought to be ashamed of himself. I can tell you that. What the hell's the matter, hasn't he got a libido?

RONNIE

I don't know if you're proud of him for——

DOUGLAS

Proud of what?

RONNIE

Well, he doesn't drink, he doesn't scoot around on a motor-cycle, he's no——

DOUGLAS

Well, maybe he should! I told him he could have the car any time he wanted it. He hasn't asked for it once.

RONNIE

Well, whenever are you not using it?

DOUGLAS

Plenty is the answer to that, plenty.

RONNIE

You also told him you'd get him a new Austin. He hasn't seen that.

DOUGLAS

Not on your damn life until he shows some interest. What am I going to get a car to rust in the driveway?

(*Somewhat to the audience.*)

Took him out to the damn lot, looked around mildly, came back saying he liked them all, and started taking a bus to school; what the hell?

RONNIE

Well, I don't want to argue.

ALAN

When would I have time?

RONNIE

That's what I said, Alan. Still.

ALAN

I can't see it's any of his business, anyway, good God.

RONNIE

I told him he didn't have a detective on your tail, how did he know?

ALAN

Tail is funny. Oh, well.

DOUGLAS

(*Continuing with Ronnie.*)

When I was his age, I knew the score all around. I'm not going to break him in like a hunting dog: stick a quail in his mouth and have him spit it out till I can teach him what it is. He isn't stupid. What kind of man doesn't know where the hunt is? Huh? I don't want to tell you! It just isn't living. Life is for living, Ronnie. The Best Is None Too Good.

ALAN

(*Rather rapidly.*)

I'll bet a hundred times Mom's told me that: "Your dad always said, 'The best is none too good, the best is none too good.'" She used to say I was like him a lot—"You're like him a lot"— and she was right, dammit, more right every day I live——

DOUGLAS

No, by God, he isn't . . . like me! Not on your life he isn't. Maybe I got into trouble and maybe I got with some kids that were a bad influence—I don't say I was an angel—but I knew where the food was and where my hands were and my mouth and my cock and my belly; and if I knew what I had, I knew where to put it, too. And I had women. I mean real women. Hell, the first woman I had was thirty-five years old and I was a kid fifteen, and don't think she didn't teach fast. Hell, I'm younger now than he is. And I grew up in the same goddamned two-bit Nebraska town he did; so don't pull that.

RONNIE

I don't think it's at all unusual for a boy seventeen to be more——

DOUGLAS

I don't want to hear it. I'm younger now than he is now. You squeal around a corner with the girl's hair flying out, by God, and she's all over you. Wiggling her behind in your lap, by God; you pull over to the curb and let 'em have it right there. You pull into a garage. Or a lot, a parking lot. What's he going to do, take a cheap bottle of booze up to some wet hotel room? What does he know? I never went to one cheap hotel room with a bottle of cheap booze in my life. You think I'm going to sit on those sway-backed mattresses, burn-holes all over the furniture varnish? Glass circles. God knows what laid what there. Out in the damn grass alongside the road under nature's clean sky with the wind blowing and *stars!* All that smell of lipstick. Hell, the beaches at night are lined up; where's he? Huh? Goddammit, he's eighteen years old; what's he doing, jerkin' off?

RONNIE

Well, tell him, honey; don't tell me—I'm not interested in seducing young girls.

DOUGLAS

His mother stunted him. Neutered him. He's humiliating. Just looking at his damned—all right, he's a damn-all-right-looking guy, or could be. There's nothing wrong with him. He's let those two damn phony girls twist his hair up like a pretzel, all curled up like some kind of rock 'n' roll singer.

RONNIE

That's what the girls are going for nowadays, I guess.

DOUGLAS

Oh, shit, Ronnie. Nowadays. Hair that long, curled up like that, I can hardly sit at the table with him without throwing up! I'd like to snatch him bald—nowadays! Women go for men and that's all! Women go for vitality, vigor, exuberance, strength. Balls, for God's sake. What are you talking? Huh?

ALAN

You know——

DOUGLAS

Huh?

ALAN

——Dad asked me——

DOUGLAS

Aw, hell, go on!

(*Exits.*)

ALAN

——last night to contribute twenty-five dollars each week to the family fund. To pay my way around here . . . for room and board. For twelve years he didn't pay a red cent to my welfare, and suddenly I'm a drain on the budget. Another mouth to feed. Goddamn. I found out what the mortgage on the house is——

RONNIE

Well, I told you that. It isn't a secret, surely.

ALAN

A hundred and three dollars a month.

RONNIE

For twenty years, though.

ALAN

Unless you pay it off sooner, and you're paying a hundred twenty, which is what the two girls bring in—they just sign over the checks to the mortgage, *actually!*

RONNIE

That isn't even what they eat.

ALAN

(*To the audience and Ronnie.*)

I didn't believe it. . . . And he wants a hundred-plus a month from me as my contribution to the gas and food. I don't feel I should be working for you . . . down there for you. All I bargained for was part-time work and full-time college. I'm full-time working and I can't save the money to quit work because you people can't afford to keep me here unless I pay my own way!

RONNIE

Don't you think you should pay toward it? Because we can't. We'd like you to know that.

ALAN

I didn't think I should pay. I quite frankly didn't think I should pay. I worked down there with noise that would bring down mountains seven hours a day, when I could pull myself together after school to go, and I didn't really mind if it was doing something. All right, we're all of us selfish. If I was using it for tuition and books and school—but paying the rent on Dad's house!

RONNIE

(*Suddenly. Quietly and seriously.*)

You're an equal member of the family, Alan. The inheritance will be divided three ways equally between Doug's three kids; you'll get just as much as the kids do.

ALAN

(*Thrown.*)

What? Well, that's a long time off—what kind of talk? Anyway——

RONNIE

I just want you to feel—I want you to know that, Alan. Truly.

DOUGLAS

(*From the other side. Quite heatedly and suddenly joining them. He has taken up a lunch pail and a pocket holder for pencils with a red and green badge on it, which he carries in his shirt pocket.*)

Stay where? By God, when I say come on to work, I mean it. What the hell have—where are you sick?

ALAN

All over. I'm not sick; I don't feel like working. I don't feel well. I don't want to go. I have things to do; I don't feel good—well.

DOUGLAS

Stanley tells me you're never there five days a week. At least when you're home frisking around all day like today, by God, you can go to work. Since when didn't you feel well?

ALAN

Since now. What's wrong? What difference does it make?

DOUGLAS

Listen here, mister; if schools gets in the way, then you can quit school. I don't see work getting in the way of school. Are you missing there too? Huh?

ALAN

No, not yet.

DOUGLAS

You mope around like a sick calf; now it's about time someone put a firecracker under your tail. See if there's any life in you. You and Penny—the whole lot of you. Maybe you should take liver tablets or something.

ALAN

(*With some humor.*)

Perhaps I should. What's wrong; can't I be sick?

DOUGLAS

If I believe it. There's no goddamned reason why you can't go in except you don't want to. . . . By God now, Alan, and I'm serious, I just want to know one thing——

ALAN

Why should I? Of what importance is the job down——

DOUGLAS

Because I told you to. I said so. . . . I told you to get ready, I wasn't having you make the whole damn carload of us late again. Now, are you coming or not?

ALAN

No, goddammit! I'm not. That's what I said. I don't feel well. I've got three chapters to read on——

DOUGLAS

Listen here! Now, once and for all. I'm not going to say this twice now; this has been coming. Do you want to stay here? Answer me!

ALAN

(*Letting down, relaxing.*)

Yes, that's what I've been saying. I told you. It's as simple——

DOUGLAS

I mean, do you want to *stay* here? Live here? In this house?

ALAN

(*Quite thrown.*)

What? I guess so. Yes—what—yes, of course I do.

DOUGLAS

(*Very strongly.*)

Then, by God, if you do, you better know this is my home. And I say here. I call the shots here, and what I say goes, mister. And those that don't like it can find a roof over their heads somewhere else. And you better be for learning that fast. Because I don't take any shit. None.

ALAN

I know—that——

DOUGLAS

None! Mister! Not from you or anybody else, huh? And you better be for learning that fast!

(*Exits.*)

ALAN

(*Standing where he was. Tries to speak to the audience. Very upset, trying to be rational.*)

I—my whole body—hell, I can't do—was pounding. Well, I hadn't—he left. I—I—Ronnie went down the hall.

(*She does.*)

And into—I went out—blindly turned around and went out into the back yard.

(*He does.*)

And fell down on the ground and bawled like I never remember bawling before or since. Sobbing. I—I—

(*Fighting for objectivity.*)

Now, what was going through my—what was I thinking? Well, of course, all the times I had wanted a father and not had one. The times I had wanted to live with Dad. The struggle Mother had had during the war, working in a garment factory. And before that, the little I could remember—of—remember of Dad, before. And what I had been told, Mom's stories. And my sister, who had been born dead while he was out with—whomever it was he was out with. That had always been my picture of him: Mom walking the floor, him coming in and her crying—

Ronnie was in the house. I was very aware of that. I expected her to come out and talk to me. Something. Ronnie and I were close—friends.

If I had left. Then. Where would I have gone? I couldn't consider it. This is where I had come to—right to the edge of the continent. I didn't think about going. I couldn't leave. I didn't know what we had been fighting about. I honestly didn't; not then.

Well, neither here nor there. Finally I got up. Aching. And went inside.

RONNIE

I knew you went out. I knew you were crying. I didn't look out. I assumed you wanted your privacy. I wasn't going to embarrass you.

ALAN

(*A kind of laugh.*)
Humf.

RONNIE

I just sat. Tried to sort the wash, not to listen, cleaned up the bedroom. Penny had vanished—very unlike her—nobody had seen her all afternoon. Rose finally called at eleven and said she was over there, which was all right, I suppose; at least we knew where she was.

ALAN

I went to bed about twelve. Dad came home after work. I heard him in the kitchen making scrambled eggs, I suppose, or French toast. I almost expected him to come in and apologize. All right, I did expect him to. I don't know for what. I couldn't sleep. I got up and dressed after he'd gone to bed. Actually went to a bar. Deserted bar.

RONNIE

And came home drunk as a lord.

ALAN

You shouldn't have stayed up.

RONNIE

I woke up and wondered where you'd gone.

ALAN

The next morning, bright and early, Dad's photography club

went off to the mountains. And I woke up with a hangover—so we begin and end, both, with a splitting headache. And Penny came home to leave.

PENNY

(*Ending a very long cross to Ronnie during the above.*)
Ronnie? Ronnie?

RONNIE

What, Pen?

PENNY

Could I talk to you alone?

RONNIE

How come you stayed with Rose, Penny? You should call when you decide to leave like that; we were worried abo——

PENNY

I can't stay here. I love you very much, but I'll go live with Rose. I've already asked them and they said it was all right. I didn't tell them why—I wouldn't tell them that—I——

RONNIE

What's wrong, Penny? You know you can't live with Rose, Penny; that's stupid.

PENNY

With her mother, I can live with her mother. She can take me. Ronnie, yesterday afternoon—with Doug—we were in the darkroom—we were just standing there and—like always, working—and he put his arm around me, and he started talking to me about—talking to me about how I liked to help him and about how good a foster father he'd been to me and what a good relationship we had, and he kissed my cheek. I didn't know what to do. I thought of once when I was about fourteen a man tried to put his hand in my lap in a movie once. I felt the same way, and he put his hand up under my shirt, on my stomach, and tried to turn me around and kiss my mouth—with his mustache on my cheek, and I—I just pulled away and got out—went out. (*Beat. Then she catches her breath.*)

RONNIE

Well, don't cry; you're O.K., aren't you?

PENNY

I want to leave here.

RONNIE

Well, I don't blame you, honey—but you don't have to do that, Penny, my God. The sky didn't fall in, Henny Penny.

PENNY

What will he do? I can't look him in the face, Ronnie. I'm going to pack now because I don't want to sleep here. You can tell the authorities that I'm still here if you want to, and they won't know the difference; they never care anyway. I don't want to tell them why.

RONNIE

Oh, Penny, stop being so much. It's all too pathetic. I mean, damn. It's just stupid.
(*To the audience.*)
I mean, Penny, for God's sake. Look at her. She hasn't a single quality anyone would go for unless you happen to really desire pure virginity in the abstract. I mean I know her qualities, but you couldn't expect Doug to see them.

PENNY

Ronnie, I don't want to leave.

RONNIE

I said you didn't have to——

PENNY

I hate Rose! She's fat and stupid and she talks too much and I hate her boyfriends—they *all* have beards and——
(*Now she does cry, and quite loudly, openly.*)

RONNIE

All right, *do* cry if you want to. Go on. It's absurd. Don't be silly.

JACK

(*Entering, Carol just behind.*)
What's wrong with Penny?

CAROL

(*Entering.*)
Come on, buster.

JACK

What's wrong?

CAROL

Where do you want me to start?

RONNIE

Jack, honey, go on outside.

CAROL

(*Exits with Jack.*)

Come on, loverboy . . .

PENNY

Why did he do that?

RONNIE

I don't know. You're not going to leave now, Penny. You don't have to see him if you don't want to. It's only six months, Penny; don't be silly.

PENNY

Why did you tell him? You knew what he'd say. You're very bright. Why the hell did you tell him, Ronnie?

RONNIE

Penny, I'd always known pretty much what to expect from Doug. I wasn't worried about him being brought up for rape charges by those girls he ogles over; sublimation is a wonderful thing. As long as it works.

(*To the audience.*)

But to make a creepy pass at Penny! It hadn't entered my mind. What was he trying to prove?

(*Back to Penny.*)

And you wanted to crawl away, and do you think he wouldn't know why? Doug—if the heat gets too hot—will just pick up and leave, as you, Alan, well know. And I have two kids to think about. . . . I'm sorry, Alan; are you O.K.?

ALAN

It's O.K.

RONNIE

Now, I mean, I wonder.

ALAN

It's just as well, really.

DOUGLAS

(*Entering.*)

Well, we went up into the mountains this morning—you've never seen anything like it. Some of those——

RONNIE

If you aren't the most ridiculous, childish oaf I've ever seen!

DOUGLAS

Why's that?

RONNIE

Penny's in there hysterical; she tells me you made a dumb sloppy pass at her in the garage yesterday afternoon. If you aren't an ass—to begin with for thinking she wouldn't come immediately like a shocked virgin and tell me. Confess to me.
(*Douglas stands shocked and silent.*)
I can't believe you did something like that. I hope you don't delude yourself into thinking she liked it. She wants to leave is what she's thinking; she wants to go live with Rose. I told her it was stupid. If you don't know better than to upset a girl like that!

I swear to God, if it's true, you ought to be ashamed of yourself. I know I am for you if you're not. Or I would be, Doug, if it weren't all so laughable.
(*Beat. Beat. Douglas continues to look at her. No one moves except Carol and Alan.*)

CAROL

Well, that ought to be it then.

ALAN

I'd think.

CAROL

He says No, right?

ALAN

As best I recall.

(*Curtain.*)

Act Three

(Alan comes forward. The stage is rather dark at the beginning, growing slowly and steadily lighter.)

RONNIE
(From the darkness, faintly.)
Alan, honey, get up, Mount McGinty is on fire, the whole sky's——

ALAN
The greatest sight while I stayed in California was something that the Californians *do* fear. Their homes, many of them—and many of the nicer ones—range up into the brush and forests in the mountains. In the fall, when it's dry—even for here—bone dry, dead, fires light the sky. Mount McGinty and Otay in the distance burned. The sky was red. The mountains were ochre with dried grass and brush one day and that night streaked with red fire and the next morning black. Houses were destroyed, timber and game and the view.

Along about this time a poet—of local fame at school—who had left State a few years earlier, came back for a day or so. I have tried to remember what he wrote, but outside of a firm conviction that he was the most brilliant person I'd ever met, and wrote more perfectly than—oh, skip it. I can't remember a word, in any case, and that's odd. It was probably more lines about creepy ferns and creepy shadows for creepy creeps. I do know we spoke, that we walked up into the mountains that had burned, around a landscape that looked like the moon. Charred mesquite and ashes six inches deep. The brush, some of it—the fire had gone through it so quickly, some of the brush stood—like ashes on a cigarette—stood three feet high—the white negative of the brush exactly intact, and you touched it and it disintegrated. And into the woods that were saved to commune with what was left of nature. And after three afternoons of walking I skipped two days of school to stay mostly in my room and when I went back, the poet had left—he wasn't around. It is of pertinence only as a very ironic coincidence. Ronnie said about Mount Helix: "Just like I thought, there it is."

97

Who knows what a person is made of? I promise not to tell you if you promise not to tell me. I left Nebraska to come to the promised land because I had to. I left because I had to. This is the state I'm in. California. So much is true here, so much is open; so much is honest and so much is impossible to admit. Even of what I know is there, what I realize is there. In this state.

CAROL

It's a good enough state to be in.

ALAN

"I would like to thank the theatre"? Poor bitch.

CAROL

Right. Where else am I? Nowhere.

ALAN

You're always here, in my state. With all those possibilities, if only——

CAROL

Yes, I know. "If only" is a good state.

ALAN

(*Ironically*.)

California.

CAROL

Not that it matters, when you look at it from this distance, but that week—the week of the fire—I got engaged to Sonny. We will say briefly that the marriage didn't come off and the following year, quite without me giving a damn, I became a highway statistic and about as violently as one would have expected. My date for that particular night got rather too drunk, and like the idiot he was, drove us off—it's funny—it was funny then—shot like a rocket off Inspiration Point.

ALAN

And landed in the valley below.

CAROL

Hours . . . actual hours later.

ALAN

And burst into flames.

CAROL

(*Pause.*)

If you say so.

ALAN

Ronnie wrote me—her second and last letter—some time back.

CAROL

There should be something enormous I should say—what an opportunity. I was very good that last year. No one knows. I know it doesn't seem like it. But I was so damn good. I'm not saying I'm sorry. Goddamn, I hate people who say they're sorry.

ALAN

Right.

CAROL

Once we were engaged we didn't get along—suffice it to say without ruining the story that something came up with which Sonny violently disagreed, and we told each other to fuck off.

ALAN

And your date for that particular evening, who drove you over the cliff——

CAROL

——was a clod; forget it. I was aware that we were nowhere —I mean nowhere *about* to make the corner ahead. Mountain road. And I stiffened, like I was looking for the brake on my side of the car, and not a word, not a scream. Saw it all; thought: My God, some car is going to come along and see the barrier torn up on this curve and be scared to death. Saw it all. In slow motion, if you please.

ALAN

And Sonny wasn't with you?

CAROL

How do you mean wasn't with me?

(*Rather bitter for just a second.*)

Well, that shows what you know, doesn't it? No, Sonny was in downtown San Diego, right?

RONNIE

Right, or so he said.

CAROL

At the time. There. Sonny was somewhere in San Diego, or so
he said, getting drunk and listening to records. At the time.
(*Beat.*)
Which shows what he knows, doesn't it? You didn't know right
away, did you?

ALAN

No, some time. Ronnie wrote me. A reply to a request for a
loan of money.

CAROL

You don't tell me your dreams, Alan, and I won't tell you mine.

ALAN

Deal.

CAROL

Deal.

RONNIE

Doug is an excellent provider, Alan; you can't see it, I know,
but he is. And I'm an excellent manager, all considered. And I
have Jerry and Jack, and they are more important to me than
anything in the world.
(*Proudly.*)
The boys are quite grown, of course, and quite normal, and
I'm very proud of them. You would be, too. Jerry bowls.

ALAN

Bowls? Really? Jerry twelve. Jerry fifteen. Jerry twenty-five.
Jerry thirty. Thirty-five. Forty.
(*Nearly crying, but recovering.*)
Jerry, Jerry. And hairy Jack. It's like a cartoon strip, and after
one artist quits, another takes over and you can hardly tell the
difference—yet something—
    Quite normal? I had hoped—eccentric somehow.

DOUGLAS

To each his own, I guess.

ALAN

Deal.

DOUGLAS

Not at all eccentric. Not at all. Just ordinary.

RONNIE

In an extraordinary sort of way.

ALAN

Deal.

RONNIE

You were so drunk that night. I thought you'd faint right on the floor.

PENNY

I . . .

(*Everyone turns to her; a pause.*)

DOUGLAS

Yeah?

PENNY

I don't care, one way or the other.

RONNIE

You always wanted to be a teacher.

PENNY

Not civics, I don't think. I teach civics. I'm not good with them, really; you have to be more of a disciplinarian than anything.

ALAN

Married, right?

PENNY

Oh, yeah. Kids.

CAROL

No white coat?

PENNY

No rice, really, either.

DOUGLAS

So, all those deals, some of 'em get good cards, some of 'em——

CAROL

(*Cutting in.*)

And some of them get a lousy hand and haven't the nerve to bluff or the sense to fold. Thanks, anyway, Alan. I appreciate it. You know you hardly entered my mind. I had quite a world going for me there.

ALAN

People are always entering people's minds at inopportune times. The least I could do——

CAROL

(*Singing gently.*)

Walk right in, sit right down; Daddy, let your hair hang down. . . .

ALAN

What are you on?

CAROL

I don't even know.

PENNY

(*To Ronnie.*)

I liked Doug, really. I'd never had a father that I remembered.

RONNIE

I know, Penny.

PENNY

I didn't want to leave.

RONNIE

You didn't have to leave, Penny, my God. The sky didn't fall in, Henny Penny.

PENNY

What will he do? I can't look him in the face, Ronnie.

CAROL

God bless us, every one.

RONNIE

Yes, indeed, Carol.

ALAN

Deal. God bless us, every one. I must have drunk about . . .
(*Drunk.*)
. . . about . . . about . . .

RONNIE

Come on.

ALAN

About a keg of stale beer. I'll bet I really did. You know, California beer tastes like slop.

RONNIE

Right, no good at all; you shouldn't drink it.

ALAN

Now you tell me.

RONNIE

Why don't you go off to bed and get some sleep now before you wake up the whole house. Even Carol's in bed already.

ALAN

You go on to bed. The bartender kept sitting beers in front of me, and he knew I wasn't of age. I should report him for selling beer to a minor. I don't think he even charged me for the last couple, though. Just as soon as I finished, there'd be another one there, like the Sermon on the Mount. Bread and fishes. He says, "We have a couple of girls," and I said, "No, thank you, I just want to get very stoned. I haven't been stoned since I left Nebraska"—I haven't, you know.

RONNIE

I know.

ALAN

And he said, "Don't get sick, it's gonna be a scorcher tomorrow." He was from Kansas. There's no such thing as a native Californian.

RONNIE

I thought you wanted me to go on, and now you're talking.

ALAN

Did I make any sense?

RONNIE

Very little sense.

ALAN

I was so dizzy I couldn't even see the room. And . . . go on. . . .

RONNIE

O.K.: "Go on to bed; it'll be a good day tomorrow."

ALAN

And tomorrow came and the Kansan was closer.

PENNY

You can tell the authorities that I'm still here if you want to.
They never care anyway.

CAROL

They never gave a wild flying damn about any of us really.
Who cares about anyone?

RONNIE

It's impossible to take seriously. Penny? It's an insult to me for
one thing, which of course Penny couldn't know, but I'd expect
you to see that. I swear to God, you ought to be ashamed of
yourself; I know I am for you if you're not; or I would be
if——

DOUGLAS

(*Cutting in.*)

It's a goddamn——

RONNIE

Oh, come on, Doug, so you tried to sneak a quick——

DOUGLAS

That lying bitch—is what I'm saying. I might want her to feel
at home. Can't I put my arm around her and give her a squeeze?
Goddammit, she's never had a father! Her life—the bitch. Not
another night under my house, that bitch, if she thinks she can
accuse me of—Alan! I want to talk with you. Now this isn't
something that I want passed around, and I don't think you'll—
I don't want to see her face here again. No, by God, she can
go to Rose, she can go to hell for all I care. She's not spending
another night under my roof.

RONNIE

Doug, it doesn't matter—of course she can——

DOUGLAS

Like hell it doesn't matter. Doesn't matter! You try to show
some affection for someone—I didn't touch the tight bitch; I
didn't go near her. What's she trying to pull? And by God, if

you believe it, you can go to hell too. I won't have it. I won't
have it, by God.

PENNY

I didn't want to cause anything—why did you tell him—I'm
leaving.

DOUGLAS

The whole goddamn bunch of them can clear out for all I care.
They can get out now.

ALAN

Why did you tell him?

RONNIE

I didn't say you did; I said Penny said you did. I think it's funny;
there's nothing to get upset about. Good God, Doug.

ALAN

Why did you tell him?

DOUGLAS

No, by God, I never touched her.

RONNIE

She says you kissed her on the cheek. She didn't say any more
than that.

DOUGLAS

Well, what the hell's wrong with that, a father kissing a daughter? *If I had!* I'm supposed to be her father—she's never had
a family—what the hell would be wrong with that? If I had!
Which I didn't, by God.

RONNIE

It just isn't important.

DOUGLAS

Well, something is—Alan!

ALAN

What?

DOUGLAS

(*Very tense—more intense than shouting.*)
This is important—more than that girl—as far as I'm concerned.

ALAN

What's wrong? I've not missed work any if——

DOUGLAS

Just let me talk, if you will, please now.

RONNIE

Nothing is of such importance, Doug——

DOUGLAS

(*Overlapping.*)

I said, goddammit, I'm going to talk now. Doug is gonna talk for a change now—I might know something!

ALAN

(*To the audience.*)

He—I don't know. If I had known then what he was thinking, perhaps——

DOUGLAS

(*Whirling him around, cutting in. Overlapping.*)

LOOK AT ME WHEN I'M TRYING TO— Now you've been avoiding, conniving, and lying the whole goddamn time. Now I'm going to talk.

RONNIE

Doug, it isn't necessary to——

DOUGLAS

All right now! Penny you stay, goddammit, right there: I'll deal with your lies.

(*To Alan.*)

Jerry tells me that you and Phil have been sitting out at the cliffs in his sparkling Pontiac. Last night and night before that and night before that.

ALAN

With Penny and Phil, yeah. I went in to work the following day; I don't know——

DOUGLAS

That doesn't interest me! It's your job, brother; you can get fired from it if you goddamn well like—I just want to know if it's true.

ALAN

What? Is what true? I don't know what you're getting at, Dad. I haven't any idea what——

DOUGLAS

You goddamned *bas*tard, stall for time. You know, don't you?

ALAN

Well, I don't see any point in——

DOUGLAS

Yes, you are, goddammit; it all fits—everything fits; suddenly it dawns. Suddenly it dawns. Yeah, and everyone—all your friends at State know it. Well, he has to have—I'm talking about Phil; you know goddamned well what I'm saying—he has to have someone to cover for him; he can't spend *all* his time with the sailors from the queer bars downtown. Everybody else is too wise to fool. Penny wouldn't ask questions; she has to take what she can get, and she deserves just what she takes. If she's the cover-up of some rich queer, she's too stupid to ask questions . . . I feel sorry for the lying bitch if she's that stupid. But you're not dumb. I thought you had some physical problem maybe; I should have been wise, man! It's sure easy for you—going out with Penny and him. What are you—holding hands behind her back?

ALAN

Lie! That's no——

DOUGLAS

Then what are you doing?

ALAN

What are you saying?

DOUGLAS

I'm saying you're through around this house. Not with my kids —not—you're not going to make sissies out of my two boys, and you're not going to breathe in my house—not my air any more!

ALAN

That's a lie! How can you say that with Penny here? She knows better—and Jerry——

DOUGLAS

Penny knows goddamn well it's true. Look at her. Ask her if he's once tried to lay her or even thought about it. Hell, ask

Carol; Carol knows it and Ronnie knows it and every other goddamned person in the county knows it, and you do, too. He's famous. Everybody's so goddamned afraid to hurt, disillusion, little Penny's feelings—so they let her live in a dream world. He must be laughing himself silly. Hell, he must spit on her. He knows a good thing when he sees it.

ALAN

Ask Carol . . .

(*But Carol is already shaking her head, better not ask me.*)

Well, if it's *true*, what do you mean saying it? What do you mean by saying that?

DOUGLAS

(*This intense, not loud.*)

Not in my house.

ALAN

He never touched me. I don't know why you can't leave my sex interests alone or to myself.

DOUGLAS

I intend to protect my own. I'm not having it. Now, I can't take this.

ALAN

What do you mean? What are you doing?

DOUGLAS

I'm telling you to go back to where you came from—we don't need you here. It's been disturbance since you came. Now, you take your little imitation leather suitcase in there and your record player and everything you've *touched* in this goddamned house, and pack them back up into a little——

ALAN

No! By God. Damn you! I'm going to say one thing! You're lying and I don't know why! But you are and you know you are! I'm no good at this——

DOUGLAS

Well, if you think I am——

ALAN

You see! That's all I know. What you are not! You're not!

You're nothing! You think the best is none too good, and you don't have any idea at all about the best! You'll never see it! And all your lies prove!

DOUGLAS

Get out. That's all I want from you, mister, that's all. That's all. That's all—just go on. Out. That's all.

ALAN

Mur-der-er!

(*Sobbing.*)

MURDERER! I had a sister and you killed her. Killed your own daughter trying to be a man—whoring—and if that's what you want me to be like and Jerry to be like and all of us, then I may have the satisfaction.

DOUGLAS

(*Slaps him sharply across the face.*)

That's a lie! That's a lie!

ALAN

NO! You killed her! As well as if you had beat her to death. . . . Jerry's sister and Jack's sister and my sister! You drove my mother insane with your whores, and you're so proud of it! And you've come out here with her. And you're never going to forget it!

DOUGLAS

That's a goddamn lie. She never.

ALAN

She was born a bloody dead mass! Not even human! Thrown to the trash to burn, and you did it! You know it!

DOUGLAS

(*Injured; quietly.*)

How can—you have no idea—what that did to me. No idea. You'll never know as long as you live—you couldn't—you'll never—by God—have a kid to know what it's like. Now you get your things in there, and you get out of here—in half an hour. I don't care where you go. You just get out of my sight now!

(*Penny has left just before Alan's line "Murderer." She goes*

down the hall, walks to the door of the bedroom, takes Carol's
orange robe under her arm, and heads toward the bathroom.
At the door of the bathroom Carol reaches her. Penny tries to
close the door, but Carol blocks it. They struggle with the
bottle of pills. Carol's line comes now.)

CAROL

No, Penny!

PENNY

No, let me—stop—stop—stop!

CAROL

(*At the same time.*)

. . . the hell do you think you're doing goddammit—Give
THEM TO ME!

(*Penny screams. Carol is still struggling with her. The pills fly*
from the bottle across the floor, scattering all around them.
Some are in Penny's hand. Penny and Carol both go to their
knees, Carol trying to hold Penny's hands away from her
mouth, Penny trying to stuff pills into her mouth. Struggling.)
Stop it, Penny. Stopit. . . . Stopit. . . . Give them to me. What
are you trying to do?

PENNY

(*At the same time.*)

No, don't. Get away, Carol, get away. No, let me! Carol, don't.

RONNIE

(*Reaches them.*)

Penny—stop it—did she take any?

CAROL

I don't think so.

(*Jack enters.*)

PENNY

Please, please, let me!

(*Ronnie gets a strong hold on Penny; Jack picks up several of*
the pills.)

CAROL

Jack, stay away, go out! Don't touch those!

RONNIE

Jack, put those back—throw them down. Every one. Now!
(*He does.*)
What are they?

CAROL

I don't know.

RONNIE

What are they?

CAROL

Just never mind—it isn't important—they're aspirin.

RONNIE

What are they, Carol?

CAROL

I said, "Never mind"; it doesn't matter. Penny, baby, come on,
honey——

RONNIE

I said, goddammit, you tell me what they are!

CAROL

(*Screaming.*)
They're Mellaril, Mellaril, dope! What the goddamn hell do you
think they are? And I don't give a shit what——
(*Ronnie slaps her across the face. Carol immediately slaps her
back. Douglas arrives, slings Carol halfway across the stage.*)

DOUGLAS

Take them! Take them! All! Take them—every goddamn one!

RONNIE

It's all right. Carol, take care of her.

CAROL

I'm sorry. Let her take care of herself.

PENNY

I'm O.K.
(*She turns to go.*)
Leave me alone. All of you. Just don't touch me!
(*Ronnie reaches toward her.*)
Don't touch me!

(*Ronnie turns; Alan follows her. Douglas begins to pick up the pills.*)

ALAN

Ronnie. Ronnie——

RONNIE

(*Interrupting.*)

I didn't know you had had a sister who had been born dead, Alan. I'm very sorry. I don't know what to say.

ALAN

All—I shouldn't have said anything. I have—I don't know what to do, Ron; he's—nothing he said is true—I can't leave you and Jack and—what am I supposed to do? What am I——

RONNIE

I think you'd better go.

(*She walks away, toward her room.*)

DOUGLAS

(*Finishing picking up the pills. Going to her as she leaves Alan.*)

Ron—Ronnie.

RONNIE

Doug, I don't want to talk to you. I want to lie down. Where's Jerry?

DOUGLAS

He's outside.

RONNIE

I just want to lie down.

DOUGLAS

Ron—Ronnie, baby—what could I do?

RONNIE

Nothing, Doug. It's all right.

DOUGLAS

Everything's going to be all right.

JACK

(*Going to Alan.*)

Do you have to go?

ALAN

Yeah, I will.

DOUGLAS

Really. Forget it. It'll all be over. We're better off, Ronnie.

RONNIE

I'm sure, Doug. I don't want to think about it.

DOUGLAS

(*Turning, looking to him.*)

Alan? Alan, I want you to know—all those years . . .

ALAN

I know, Dad.

(*Douglas and Alan are very far apart. Jack beside Alan, Douglas by Ronnie, Jerry alone outside. Penny and Carol together near their room.*)

PENNY

Oh, God, Carol.

CAROL

It's all right, baby. Nothing matters.

JACK

I don't want you to leave; you just got here.

ALAN

It's O.K., baby.

JACK

Really, don't.

(*It begins to grow dark again.*)

ALAN

Baby, it's good to remember that someone said that. . . .

DOUGLAS

(*Calling as though across time.*)

All those years. I wanted to help. What was I supposed to do? Alan?

(*It continues to grow dark.*)

JACK

Please. Take me with you, then.

ALAN

Baby, I will. Really, don't worry. You're eight years old and a little white orangutan.

JACK

Really, though, let me go with you, Alan. Can I?

ALAN

You will, Jack; I promise.

(*Only the faintest light remains on Alan and Jack. Jacks turns to go in, leaving Alan alone in the spot.*)

DOUGLAS

Hugged me, by God. By God, you can't——

PENNY

Pleased to meet you; I've heard a lot about you.

DOUGLAS

——no matter what anybody anywhere says—you can't separate a kid from his father.

JERRY

Alan? Are you awake?

PENNY

Good night.

JERRY

Good morning.

CAROL

(*Their voices tumble over each other.*)

Thanks, anyway, Alan; I had quite a little world going for me. Walk right in, sit right down——

(*Continue to end.*)

JERRY

(*Cued by Carol's "Alan."*)

We had orange trees and plum trees and a fig tree.

RONNIE

(*Cued by "orange trees."*)

If you have faith the size of a mustard seed, you can move mountains.

(*On "faith," Alan laughs to himself.*)

DOUGLAS

(*Cued by "size."*)

I know she must have told you things about me.

PENNY
(*Cued by "told."*)
I'll probably teach; I like kids.

RONNIE
(*Cued by "teach."*)
Welcome, Alan, welcome. Hello.

ALAN
(*Crying out.*)
LIGHTS!
(*The stage lights bounce up bright and full. Everyone is still. Alan turns and walks out. They follow, urgently whispering. Douglas's is the only voice we hear clearly.*)

DOUGLAS
(*Urgently.*)
I just want you to understand, Alan.
Alan.
Alan.
Alan.
(*The stage has returned to darkness before Alan can escape them.*)

(*Curtain.*)